Lemon Juice

The confessions of a
used car dealer -
a metamorphosis.

Also by Gene Epstein

Dying For An Heir

All proceeds realized by the author from the sale
of this book go directly to charity.

Gene Epstein

Lemon Juice

The confessions of a
used car dealer -
a metamorphosis.

Copyright © 2019 Gene Epstein.

All rights reserved. No part of this book may be reproduced, stored, or transmitted by any means—whether auditory, graphic, mechanical, or electronic—without written permission of the author, except in the case of brief excerpts used in critical articles and reviews. Unauthorized reproduction of any part of this work is illegal and is punishable by law.

The acceptance of this book releases the author and all persons involved in this book from liability. IN NO EVENT SHALL THE AUTHOR NOR PERSONS INVOLVED IN THIS BOOK BE LIABLE FOR ANY DAMAGES WHETHER DIRECT OR INDIRECT, OR INCIDENTAL OR CONSEQUENTIAL, INCLUDING BUT NOT LIMITED TO LOSS OF REVENUE.

ISBN: 978-1-6847-1136-9 (sc)
ISBN: 978-1-6847-1137-6 (e)

Because of the dynamic nature of the Internet, any web addresses or links contained in this book may have changed since publication and may no longer be valid. The views expressed in this work are solely those of the author and do not necessarily reflect the views of the publisher, and the publisher hereby disclaims any responsibility for them.

Cover design: The Steve Williams Design Office

Lulu Publishing Services rev. date: 11/15/2019

DEDICATION

To my dearest wife Marlene, who has stood by my side from the day we met in 1955 and is my best friend. Nothing in life would be possible for me without her.

To my exceptional children, Ellen and Robert, whom I love dearly.

And to my parents and grandparents for their compassion for others.

Never worry that you are doing too much to help others You are doing too little if you can do more

-Gene Epstein

TABLE of CONTENTS

	Dedication	v
	Preface	ix
	Acknowledgment	xi
	Prologue	xiii
One	In The Beginning	1
Two	Mother's Little Angel	9
Three	Stepped in it	19
Four	My First Plunge	24
Five	Jail	41
Six	Back to Business	46
Seven	Marlene and Matilda	67
Eight	My First Used Car Lot	110
Nine	Northeast Autorama	143
Ten	Estate Liquidators	177
Eleven	Bored of Education	185
Twelve	Jail (again and again)	197
Thirteen	Hammertoe	227
Fourteen	Dressed to Kill	233
Fifteen	Our Buick Dealership	246
Sixteen	Where's The Money?	253
Seventeen	Schpeel-Kiss	266
Eighteen	$700 a Knight	276
Nineteen	Have a Heart?	284
	Epilogue	291

Preface

This book was written purely for entertainment purposes. Many of my notes date back to the 1970s. Some stories contained within were told to me by others, therefore, even though this book is based upon my life, by no means can I confirm beyond a doubt that **all** of these 'incidents' actually occurred. Many entries were created by secondhand information and cannot be relied upon. In addition, names have been changed to protect the identity of certain people and/or entities mentioned within. Any names in this book relating to living or deceased people are purely coincidental. Lastly, no one mentioned in this book was ever deemed guilty of any misdeeds.

Acknowledgment

My grateful appreciation, posthumously, to Jan de Hartog, a dear friend, playwright and world renowned author of many best selling novels, for his encouragement in the 1970's to have my notes published. It was Jan who suggested the title: *"Lemon Juice, The Confessions of a Used Car Dealer" for this book.*

And my deepest gratitude, posthumously, to my high school homeroom and English teacher, Mrs. Sara Joffe, for standing up for me and encouraging me to always do my very best.

Prologue

I was sitting at my desk trying to organize some credit applications and associated paperwork from the prior day's business, when out of the corner of my eye, I noticed a man in his early 50s standing by my office door. He was wearing a long black coat, which was unusual, as it was a warm, sunny day. His figure loomed large and blacked out much of the light that normally filtered through my glass door.

I motioned for him to come in. That was my first mistake. He slowly and quietly approached the desk where I was seated. He then leaned over my desk and from somewhere inside his coat, pulled out a large caliber revolver and pointed it directly at my head. *"You're going to give Tommy half the profits from that Cadillac limousine sale today or else you're dead."*

That was **not** how I envisioned my morning at the office to start, but the used car business was a tough occupation to be in, as I quickly discovered.

It all started a couple of weeks earlier when I was purchasing automobiles for inventory at "NADE" National Auto Dealers Exchange in Bordentown New Jersey. Every Wednesday, since the auction's inception back in the 1950s, they ran a car auction. It was strictly for new and used car dealers. They only had a couple of lanes at the time running automobiles and

I would hustle from one lane to another trying to see which cars I could purchase that would have the greatest potential for profit.

I was 'eyeballing' a 1959 Cadillac - but as I walked around the car I saw some prior damage that was apparent to me and would be apparent to a customer. I noticed a 1961 Cadillac Fleetwood limousine in the opposite lane. It was traditional black with gray interior and was in beautiful condition. I started to bid on this car but soon realized that one of the many bidders was 'Crazy Tommy,' who I had known for several years. Years later, he would be found dead in the trunk of his Lincoln Continental in South Philly with multiple gunshot wounds. His death would be ruled an "apparent suicide."

Tommy, told me **he** wanted the car and that I should stop bidding. I told Tommy that if he wants the car more than me to just bid higher than me. He looked at me with contempt in his eye and said "I'm not bidding anymore. We are now partners in this car." I told Tommy I have only **one** partner - and it's not him. "If you want to outbid me," I replied, "then just bid higher than me." Oh, he didn't like that one bit. No one spoke to Tommy that way.

The following week I received a call from Tommy. He saw the car advertised in the Philadelphia Inquirer. A sale would have produced $1,000 in profits. He said he wanted his $500 share, since he'd heard the car had been sold. Thus, materialized the gun toting 'gentleman' - and I use the term 'gentleman' loosely - to my office door that day to collect Tommy's 'share.' I handed over $400 telling him I had 'overhead' and was entitled to a commission. When I think back on that incident, I must say, I had nerve to spare. How did I get to be like this? Well, it all started this way:

Lemon Juice

The confessions of a
used car dealer -
a metamorphosis.

Chapter One

In The Beginning

1939, April 21st. The doctor at the Jewish Hospital in North Philadelphia gave Sam Epstein a choice, one that he could not easily make. "Your wife has hemorrhaged to such an extent," said the obstetrician, "that regrettably, we can only save her or the baby. You must decide." Sam could not make that heart wrenching decision. It was a choice that few could make without facing a lifetime of grief. Yet, from deep within, he mustered the courage to make that agonizing choice:

"Doctor, you must save them both," murmured Sam.

The bill for the ten day stay in the hospital, including a private nurse, came to $75.00; that is when I was born - Eugene Herbert Epstein.

I was named after Eugene Ormandy because he was the conductor of the Philadelphia Orchestra. He held the position of directorship the longest in US history.

Lemon Juice

My brother Milton was a concert pianist and my eldest brother, Wesley, a violinist.

Both my wife, Marlene and I were "Knighted," by the Order of St John, Knights of Malta, for my philanthropic works. Yes, I have done relatively well in life and early on I knew it was important to "give back," to those who were less fortunate than myself. I contribute as much as possible to a variety of charitable organizations, however, I wasn't born with a silver spoon in my mouth. Far from it. As you will come to see, I started life in humble beginnings. If you would like to know how I went from being impoverished to becoming a benefactor, funding many charitable projects, I will reveal how my life evolved, which brought me to this place in time. It is somewhat akin to a modern day Horatio Alger story, but with unusual twists and turns along the way however, on a much smaller scale.

My mother's parents were an integral part of our lives. They were so loving and caring, that it made for a very close knit family growing up.

My mother, Matilda "Bille" Lipschutz-Epstein was born on January 17, 1906 in Philadelphia, PA. Her parents were Max and Roscia (later known as "Rosie") Lipschutz. They were the proud parents of seven children. My mother had an exceedingly close and loving relationship with her parents.

Her older sister, Isabelle, died when my mother was only three years of age. Her mother would tell her that Isabelle was "*the most beautiful child in the whole world,*" whom my grandmother loved dearly and grieved very hard at her loss.

In The Beginning

My mother was the middle child, and was doted upon. Frankly, I doubt her mother thought Matilda could have done anything wrong in her eyes. It was a warm and loving home in which to grow up.

My maternal great-grandfather, Jacob Lewis Axelrod, who was a lawyer, worked with two or three Counts in Germany. The Counts' offices were on the palace grounds but not situated inside the palace. One day, my great-grandfather overheard rumblings amongst the Counts that they intended to start pogroms (war) on the Jews. My great-grandfather was shocked. He didn't say anything to anyone, but waited to see what would happen. Soon afterward, the same thing happened. My great-grandfather said to my great-grandmother, *"Marsha, we're going to pack up and go to America."* And there was no further discussion about this decision. They left Germany and landed in America around 1894.

They bought a house on Fifth and Federal Streets in Philadelphia, PA. In residence with them were my great-uncles, Samuel, Morris, Joe, my great-aunts, Goldie and Yetta (Etta) and my maternal grandmother, Roscia (Rosie).

My grandmother Rose came from a wealthy family. The Axelrods were in the smelting business. The name of the business was "Girard Smelting and Refining Company."

My mother's paternal grandfather, Avrum Velvel Lipschutz, came from Lithuania to live in Philadelphia. He was a well known custom-shoemaker, whose work was so superior, that people came from great distances to have him fashion

Lemon Juice

custom-made shoes for them. One day, a group of young ruffians wandered into his store - and for no apparent reason - beat Avrum to death. It was a great shock to the community, especially to those who loved him.

My mother's youngest brother, Bernard, who was 6 feet tall, was an excellent swimmer, yet, one day he went swimming in the Delaware River and drowned. Another family tragedy.

My maternal grandparents were incredibly nice people. My grandmother, Rose, was a stately, lovable woman and my grandfather, Max Lipschutz, had blue eyes and brown hair with a wiry build and was artistically inclined. He loved drawing comics. Max, originally was a furniture dealer, but later operated a candy store that sold ice cream, newspapers and other 'convenience' items which at that time was termed "Patent Medicines." For years, his wife Rose, ran a restaurant for the employees at Girard Smelting iron foundry.

One day a drunk wandered into my grandfather's candy store insisting that my grandfather give him a light for his cigarette. Max gave him a match but the drunk insisted that my grandfather light the cigarette for him. The drunk who had earlier consumed an entire bottle of Bay Rum aftershave lotion and who now was broke, kept insisting: "Come on Max, give me a light." Max had a short temper. He was thinking to himself that 'if this man asks one more time to light his cigarette, I'm going to punch him in the nose.' To make things worse, the drunk now said "Come on Jew, gimme a light!" My grandfather mumbled something in Yiddish, then punched the drunk with such force, that the drunk's body went flying right through the plate glass window. Within minutes, the police arrived along with an ambulance. Max was arrested. The drunk was hurriedly taken away by ambulance to a hospital, where he was sewn together. I called a plate glass company to come replace the broken window. Boy oh boy, being in business was sure exciting! And to top it off, that day the store took in an extra $10.00!!!

I don't have very many remembrances of my father's parents, Nathan and Freida, although, I recall they lived less than a mile from our home in Logan. They would always give me a quarter and an apple, but more than that, I don't remember much about them.

Recently, I performed research to discern more information about Nathan and Freida Epstein. According to the 1910 Census, my paternal grandfather was born in 1872 and immigrated to the USA from Russia in 1889.

He married "Freda" (Frieda) and had eight children: Jennie, the eldest, Abraham N, Irving R, Samuel, Anna (also known as Hannah), Sylvia or Sophia(?), Judith (Judah) and Josuha who was the youngest. From this information, I can see Nathan and Freda were quite busy on those cold winter nights.

The 1910 Census records their address as 1738 North Fifteenth Street, in the 47th Ward of Philadelphia. Nathan was a tailor who worked from home. He was a Naturalized Citizen. He died on 25 February 1943 at the age of 71 of a coronary. More than this scanty information about my father's side of the family, I do not know.

Lemon Juice

One thing I do know - is that from an early age I was *unusual*.

My mother was hoping that I would become an exceptional musician since I always loved sitting in the wingback chair for hours everyday listening to my brother, Mickey, practicing on the piano for upcoming concerts.

When I was 11 or 12 years old my mother gave me two dollars to give to a piano teacher one mile from my house. I went to the first lesson and was bored. I went a second time without a better result. I suddenly had an idea. I offered the piano teacher one dollar to state that I was there and I took the other dollar went to the Logan Movie Theater and watched 26 cartoons for 10¢ and then for 55¢ I had a full course meal at the Chinese restaurant only doors away. Then, I took public transportation back to my house. That went on for about a month until I was found out.

Given the choice to sink or swim I quickly learned how to swim. Nothing was easy for me however the chances of me being born were slim to none, yet I made it into life. I was an 'angel,' as far as my mother was concerned, no matter what devilish things that I did. She was there to give me confidence that I could do anything I set my mind to do. I was really a devilish kid. That has not changed even in my advanced years.

At that time, we lived in the Logan section of North Philadelphia and my father, Sam, was very prosperous compared to most anyone in the neighborhood. He exported used tires to China and India and for business purposes, kept an apartment in the Waldorf Astoria in New York City.

In The Beginning

My father had a shipment of tires heading to China. The ship just left port. By the time my father presented his Bill of Lading for payment, Civil War had broken out in China and the banks would not honor his receipt. He lost $100,000 in the 1940's and he was broke.

Returning home, my father applied for a job at Sears Tire Department. He was offered his choice between being a manager of the department for a salary of $65.00 a week, which was a decent salary for that period of time. Or start a route with no salary - only commissions. He chose the latter.

My father went to all the dealers that he knew and cultivated many additional dealers. His payment vouchers averaged $225.00. Not $225.00 total payment but that was the amount that was withheld for taxes. Sam was making about $700.00 per week, ten times the amount his boss was earning!

At 47 years of age Sam had multiple strokes. His entire left side was paralyzed. I remember visiting him at the Graduate Hospital unable to move on his left side. He saw me an he smiled "How's the 'runt' doing?" He said with pure love. My Dad's $40,000 was used up paying medical bills. We were behind with all our bills. Out of desperation my mother contacted Sam's oldest brother who was in the paper box and container business, asking for $800.00 to pay her husband's medical bills. Her request was denied. She was devastated. As I write this I don't know if she ever told my father about this incident.

Lemon Juice

One evening with the radio blaring from the middle bedroom, I could hear the theme song of "Death Valley Days," presented by "20 Mule Team Borax." At 10:30 that evening during the show, my father half-paralyzed and recognizing his lamentable prognosis, got hold of my oldest brother's US Army service pistol and took his own life, knowing that he had a $20,000 life insurance policy to hold the family together.

I was not permitted to attend his funeral and stayed at home. My mother told me afterwards there were so many people that attended his funeral, she didn't know who most of them were. Many of them told her that Sam had been sending them money to help get them through troubled times.

My father was generous to a fault and I vowed to myself to follow in his admirable footsteps. As I look back on my childhood, I realize that situation drove me to do everything possible to make sure that my family would never, ever be put in that position again.

Chapter Two

Mother's Little Angel

When I was three years old I loved watching fires. We had just moved from 5100 8th Street to the corner home which was larger. Some of the furniture had already been moved into the ground floor entrance when I found a pack of matches and started playing with them. Before too long, there was a fire in my house! It was put out quickly, however I remember hearing yelling: "My beautiful new home what did you do?!!" I had my ass beaten - and deservedly so.

I loved chocolate circle cookies and everyday along with my large glass of milk, I would have several of them to dunk into the milk. My mother had to buy extra packages of circle cookies because I would not eat them without giving some to my playmates.

I attended Birney Elementary School at Ninth and Lindley, one short block from my home. There was a March of Dimes program going on in schools and children were given a cardboard foldout that had slots in it for dimes. Each child was asked to see if they could get their parents or friends to

Lemon Juice

put in a dime hoping to eventually fill both sides with dimes. My second grade teacher handed me a cardboard foldout to bring home. I went into my mother's pocketbook and removed all her dimes to fill the slots. The next day I handed them to my teacher. She immediately contacted my mother. "Do you know that Eugene brought in his March of Dimes folders filled up in just one day?" My mother did not know since I never asked her. "He knows that my pocketbook is open and if he felt that someone needed the money more than us, then that is fine." You see, I was her 'angel' and she was my Mom.

At the age of eleven, I went to the Logan Movie Theatre one mile from our home for the Saturday matinee that featured 26 cartoons for 10¢ admission. As an incentive to bring in audiences to fill the movie theater, the theatre had a Duncan Yo-Yo contest, plus door prizes. The main prize was a pair of sneakers from Edelman's Shoe Store on Eleventh Street. I met my cousin Ricky at the movie theatre. His parents were impoverished. Ricky was about a year younger than me. I had good luck that day and won the door prize. They handed me a coupon for a pair of sneakers. I was excited. At the same time I felt bad for my cousin whose shoes had worn through to the soles. I asked Ricky to come with me to the shoe store and tried to 'prep' him to say his name was Gene Epstein. I didn't realize it did not make any difference who turned in the coupon, but I still was eleven years old and I was really scared thinking that he would say his name is Ricky Fishman and not Gene Epstein.

Mother's Little Angel

Everything went well. They never even asked for his name, which was a relief to me because he probably would've said Ricky Epstein. He left with new sneakers and walked home. I walked back to my home smiling knowing I had done a good deed.

Across the street from home was Morris and Mickey's Grocery Store and at Ninth Street, which was only 500 feet away from Axe's Grocery Store.

We were still going to Morris and Mickey's Grocery Store to buy *Lekvar* which is basically prunes smashed to smithereens.

On Sunday morning I would go to the grocery store to pick up lox [*smoked salmon*]. Morris was known to cut the lox and trim it well. I wanted him to cut the lox from the belly, which was the fattiest part and most desirable section of the salmon. As he sliced the lox and trimmed off the 'fleagle' [*wing*], a delicacy, I would ask him to cut the strip attached to the wing and charge me 10¢. To him, it was 10¢ for scrap. For me, the way Morris cut the wing with the strip attached, was used by my mother to make a delicious potato soup! I loved eating the strip attached to the wing. Even today, a lifetime later, I eat my lox and plenty of salmon almost daily and specify that it must come from the belly of the salmon.

We seldom went to the store on Ninth Street but they also owned a luncheonette at the corner of Fifth and Pike in North Philadelphia. That place was called "Cherries Luncheonette." I remember speaking with the owner. He told me that they were tired of operating both locations because it was hard for him

Lemon Juice

to get help at his other luncheonette. I was only 12 years old, nevertheless I asked him for a job. Before you know it I was taking the trolley car on Fifth Street to their location. This was in the summertime and I arrived there about 9:00 A.M, and worked till 4 o'clock. At noon, when there was a rush, I was taking orders from the customers making steak sandwiches, hamburgers, grilled cheese plus anything that was on or off the menu.

After one week of working alongside one of the owners, they asked if I felt comfortable enough to take care of the place until they returned at 4 o'clock. I had absolutely no problem with that and really enjoyed doing it.

I'm not sure if I was 12 years old or 13 but, I do recall my mother purchasing a Sears brand Craftsman bandsaw with a 12 inch neck for my birthday. I read the directions, assembled the unit and could not wait until I found some wood to cut.

I walked to the local lumberyard, about three quarters of a mile away, and spent about one or two dollars for some pine planks. I had no idea what I would do with them, but how many things are there for a 12 or 13 year old boy to think about?

I had stopped by Logan Hardware, which was about three quarters of a mile from my house, trying to think of something that I could do with my new bandsaw.

I noticed the hardware store had numerical address signs that people would nail onto the face of their houses or hammer the signs with a tapered post into the ground. To me, it seemed to be a very simple thing to make, so I tried to produce one.

I made the first sign for my house with the number "801" but I did not put the address "Lindley Avenue" on the sign since there would not be sufficient space for all those letters. Plus, it would be too costly to purchase all those extra metal letters.

After realizing how easy it would be to make one, I varnished one of the signs and brought it to Logan Hardware to ask the owner how much he was willing to pay for my handmade signs. At that time he was agreeable to paying 50¢ each and he would in turn sell them at retail for a $1.95 each; a good profit on his part.

The next day I dropped off a half-dozen signs for which he paid $3.00. I made about $2.00 in profits. This was fun since I was getting experience on the bandsaw and covering my expenses for the purchase of the wood and varnish, hoping that he would want more.

Since I had a newspaper delivery route, I was making a few dollars a week delivering newspapers and now, hopefully, I would have a little additional income from the sales of these wood signs.

Somewhere, I found a piece of masonite, which is basically compressed hardwood. I cut it into the shape of a sign and placed it on the back of my porch which stated: "Gene's Bicycle Shop." I was hoping that some of my neighbors' children's bicycles would need repair.

Lemon Juice

Everyone that needed a bicycle fixed would usually take it to Wetzel's Bike Shop on Fifth Street, but I was closer. Just like any good business person, I stopped by Wetzel's to check out my competition. I wanted to know how much they charged to fix flats, adjust spokes on the wheels, adjust Bendix brakes - and what they charged to compound and wax bicycles. To my surprise, they did not perform compounding, nor wax the bicycles, so I saw that as an opening. Knowing their prices, when neighbors stopped in asking how much I would charge to fix a flat, I made sure my prices were 50% less than Wetzel's.

Within a couple weeks I was busy making address signs to sell at wholesale prices to Logan Hardware, delivering newspapers for the Evening Bulletin and repairing a couple of bicycles a week. I remember one neighbor coming in with her son's bicycle. I charged 85¢ to compound and wax the fenders, spokes and the bicycle frame. I suggested that they get new pedals while the bicycle was there, for only an additional 85¢, which included parts and labor. I would then hop on my bicycle, ride to Penn Jersey Auto Supply, buy a pair of pedals for 45¢, then pedal back home as quickly as possible and install the new pedals on my customer's bicycle. That was the beginning of my entrepreneurial enterprises.

I continued using the bandsaw to rebuild the entire porch since the wood had rotted and could not be used, for it was unsafe. At the time we could not afford to pay a contractor to build a new porch, so I took my four wheel Radio Flyer wagon and walked to the lumberyard, brought enough lumber back for steps, railings and so forth making numerous trips in the process. I remember positioning the iron post into the ground, then testing the porch after it was done, hoping that I wouldn't fall through. The refurbished porch lasted in good serviceable condition for over 20 years. The reason I know this is because I've visited the neighborhood many years after we moved and the porch was still in use.

I did useful and helpful things in my childhood, but it's obvious that from time to time I would also get myself involved in a bit of mischief. Like the time there was a very large brick building located directly across the street from our house that was used as an indoor storage garage. It had an auto repair shop and and storage for neighbors that had the luxury of owing a second automobile with no place to park it on the crowed streets.

The side that faced our home was divided into large areas of glass window panes in framings about 8 feet wide and 6 feet high. The glass panes were embedded with a sort of chicken wire and the glass was muted so one could not see through. I don't know why anyone would wish to peer through the panes only to see about 50 cars sitting in a darkened area that gave off the smell of old oil and grease.

Being somewhat inventive and not wanting to ask my mother to buy me a slingshot, I took a coat hanger and I fashioned my own slingshot. I took eight rubber bands, doubled them up using four on each side with a piece of leather two inches wide by and inch high. It was a sturdy little slingshot! I developed incredible accuracy and constantly tried to improve my aim.

Lemon Juice

After practicing with stones and/or pebbles, I noticed the rounder pebbles were more accurate than the jagged shaped stones. Further improving my aim, I started using marbles. These projectiles were perfect for accuracy.

I snuck into the middle bedroom on the second floor of my home and opened the window about 10 inches high. From there, I practiced by picking out a particular window and focusing on that one. Each individual pane was about 12 inches wide by approximately 16 inches high, making it a good target. I placed a marble in the leather sheath, pulled back and took aim. Released. Thwack! That was the sound of success. Now that I could hit the window almost 75 feet away, my next objective was to see if I could hit a window in the center, not being satisfied by simply hitting one window. I had to stop because my mother was calling me, her angel.

The physical structure of the garage showed three peaks on the roof as if it was built in sections. Not finding anything around to practice with my slingshot I waited until my mother was listening to the radio again in the early evening.

I went into the middle bedroom and quietly opened the window. I turned the lights out in the bedroom in case someone would see me. I picked out a couple of the windows and took aim. Right on target. Thwack! But then trouble was heading my way. A couple of the nighttime porters, who heard the penetration of their wired windows, slowly walked around the perimeter of the building facing our house. Obviously, I stopped and remained ducked down in my position on my knees not touching the window fearing the sound may get their attention. Each of them had a flashlight moving it in every direction around the building looking to catch someone.

This now became a game for me. My next shot was at the top peak but I didn't want to penetrate the roof so I shot one without full force, simply to have it hit the roof and roll around. One porter pointed to the other and motioning to the top of the roof, as they started to believe they now would catch the person who was up to no good.

The first house on the street appeared to be attached to the garage. The porters walked up to the first house and from there, they climbed onto the roof. I took this opportunity to take out another marble - but this time a much larger one - loaded it into my slingshot and propelled it over to the second peak. It immediately got the porters attention. They looked as if they were soldiers on a mission. They both crouched down and used hands signals pointing to the second peak. They knew in their hearts they were were going to catch the culprit(s) very shortly.

I stopped shooting - not fearing being caught - but because I wanted to extend this game for another day.

During the day I took a close-up look at my targeted window panes. It looked like I hit the bullseye of the target. Another night while my mother was listening to one of her favorite radio stations hosting the news, was Gabriel Heater. He spoke with a deep and solemn voice that to me seemed scary. I picked out two windowpanes closer to the front office where the night attendants sat smoking cigarettes. I wanted to limit the amount of target practice since I wanted the attendants to hear that noise and react the same way. They did.

Walking outside once again around the perimeter of the building with their flashlights, they started heading to the adjacent home following my second round of marbles on the roof. I would take one more marble shot and forever stop. *'What would be my last target?'* ran through my head.

They checked out the first area peak and then went to the next peaked section, when all of a sudden I saw my target. One guy dropped his flashlight and bent over to pick it up. There, with the moon reflecting down on the roof, was one big ass. He was facing away and so I selected the right cheek. One small marble had been loaded waiting for the release… Thwack!! They never went back on the roof and my mother's little angel never did it again.

Chapter Three

Stepped in it

Coming from a family with a lineage in the automobile business both new and used, as a 12-year-old kid peering out the window from my home in Logan, I was able to identify every automobile that passed by, including the year, make and model. My brother Wesley always brought home a different automobile that was traded in at various places where he was employed. Like every other kid getting close to 16 years old (which was the youngest a person could obtain a drivers license), everyday seemed to take forever waiting to get my driver's permit. Finally my permit arrived.

When my 16th birthday arrived, we were living above a candy store that my mother and I operated call "Tabor Sweetshop." At that time my brother was driving a 1953 Pontiac Chieftain convertible, powder blue exterior with a black top and a darker shade of blue interior. The car was a straight eight cylinder engine with automatic transmission and I believe power steering. "Bummie," my brother Wesley's nickname, let **me** drive it every available moment that he had so that I

Lemon Juice

would get used to driving automobiles and hopefully pass my driver's road test. The car was gorgeous. I do remember that the automatic transmission did have a hesitation between one of the gears. My brother paid $1,100 for the car when he purchased it from his friend in our old neighborhood of Logan.

One day after I had learned how to drive correctly and parked very well, Bummie threw a set of keys to me. I still can see the yellow-orangey plastic used car dealer key fob with the keys attached floating through the air as I grabbed them with my right hand. "Happy Birthday. This is your birthday present!" I was jumping for joy because all along I knew that this car was going to be mine. I went to take the keys to hop into the Pontiac convertible when my brother asked me what I was doing. I told him I wanted to take my new car for a drive. "The Pontiac is not your car. Your car is in front of the house." I looked at the identification on the key fob which was written "1939 Plymouth." I was in a state of shock! Here I was so sure that the Pontiac Chieftain would be mine, never thinking that we certainly could not afford a car like that for a 16-year-old 'pisher.' With my head bent down I walked around a few parking spaces and parked next to the curb was a spotless 1939 Plymouth four-door sedan. I walked through the grassy area along the sidewalk and got into the Plymouth.

The interior of the car was like brand new but I was unimpressed still suffering from my letdown. I placed the key into the ignition, depressed the accelerator pedal. The car kicked over quietly and smoothly. I went to drive down to Tabor, expecting to put on a few miles. The car had absolutely no power. Through the

Stepped in it

gears it seemed slower and slower. Then there was a horrible smell permeating the entire interior. I rolled the windows down hoping to get fresh air however the smell still persisted. 'This car is a piece of shit,' went through my head. Certainly it smelled like shit.

I curtailed my test drive and brought the car back and parked in the space where I had just removed it. Bummie ask me how I liked my new birthday present and I told him that the car would not get out of its own way as if something was holding it back and that it had a terrible smell inside.

He walked over to the car and asked me if I had released the emergency brake. "Oops!" I sheepishly replied and then I noticed the smell even outside of the car. I looked down at my feet and there it was: dog shit.

When I had approached the car and walked through the grassy section adjoining the sidewalk I must have stepped in dog crap. I was embarrassed. My brother had spent his money to get me an automobile that I could use and I was unappreciative. I don't remember apologizing, but if I did not say it to Bummie back then, I would like to kick myself in the ass today.

I wasn't permitted yet to drive the car to school since I only had my learner's permit but I would take care of that very shortly. I needed someone that had a drivers license to go with me to the Belmont barracks of the State Police where I would take my driver's road test. Three kids went along with me, my

Lemon Juice

cousins Bobby Gordon, Steve and my friend Marvin, the only one with a drivers license.

Passing the test was a breeze and we all got back into the car for some reason to go to another cousin, Josh, who had a car lot on Broad Street. I pulled into his car lot with Marvin, Bobby and Steve who was Josh's son and was excited to tell him that I just got my drivers license. It was a narrow entrance to Josh's car lot but it was no problem for me to navigate. However, he insisted that I follow his directions to back the car out of his lot. He told me when to turn the wheel. I hesitated because it did not feel right, but he kept telling me back, back, back, and when I followed his directions my right rear fender hit a light pole on his property. I was furious because I felt he did that on purpose. I was also very upset that this is the first day I got my drivers license and already was in an accident within an hour. Who would believe what happened?

I took the car home and while no one was around, I rummaged through our tools and found a rubber mallet. The damage to the fender was a pressure dent and I was able to reach in between the tire and fender with the rubber mallet. I tapped it a few times and then reached in with my other hand and pushed on it as hard as I could until the dent popped out. I took some rubbing compound and after 10 minutes was able to get the surface scratches to disappear.

"So my kid brother got his drivers license and the first thing gets in an accident?" Bummie questioned me upon his arrival home. "What are you talking about?" I asked knowing full well that Josh must have told him about what happened at

Stepped in it

his lot. Then my brother said he got a call from Josh right after I hit a light pole on his property. "Take a look at the car," I said to my brother Wesley, who walked around looking at all the fenders and said "I should have never believed Josh to start with." Probably 20 years passed before I told Wesley the truth. Josh lived at 5039 N. 9th Street, which from my house in Logan was about 750 feet. His son Steve tried several times the sell automobiles from his house with no success and Josh saw that week after week I was selling cars from my house. Ironically every time that Stevie, his son, would tell him that Gene sold another car, Josh would say "He steps in shit and it turns to gold." Josh didn't know exactly how prophetic he truly was!

Chapter Four

My First Plunge

Quite often I have been asked, "How old were you when you started in the automobile business?" Tracing back through the years I know that I legally sold my first automobile at the age of sixteen when I was permitted to drive.

During my brother Wesley's tenure with a new car dealership as a salesman, he brought home a 1951 Studebaker Champion four door sedan. The car was taken in trade for $50.00 by the dealership. I promptly asked to buy it, however, I didn't have a penny. I asked my mother for the money. My mother asked me "What are you gong to do with the car if I give you the money?" Can you imagine a parent asking a sixteen year old what he or she was going to do with a car? "I don't want you to give me the money; I only want a loan because I want to buy the car wholesale and retail it quickly," I replied. Even though there was only a $86.00 balance in the checkbook and no savings accounts or cash, she somehow managed to scrape together the $50.00 I needed to buy that car and gave it to me. She was one hell of a woman to give her "runt" (that's what

My First Plunge

my dad affectionately called me), all that money. That was a huge sum in those days.

Now was my opportunity to make a buck. I proceeded to wash the heavy grease off the engine with gasoline, not knowing until months later that it could have exploded in my face. I scrubbed the upholstery and compounded and waxed the bright green finish. I immediately placed an advertisement in the local newspaper: *"1951 StudeChamp 4 door sedan, low miles. Like new. $155.00, M14435161"* **Sold!** That night the phone didn't stop ringing. There were plenty of people calling after the advertisement was cancelled. I returned the fifty dollars that I had borrowed from my mother and split the $100.00 profit with her. Now there was $136.00 balance in the checkbook.

I was now officially in the automobile business. That is, officially in my mind. I don't remember hesitating even one day to look for my next car. By the way, that old Studebaker turned out to be the best one in a long list of those that I ever sold.

I found my next car, which was an old Plymouth, and made another $100.00. Now we had $186.00 in the checkbook and I had $100.00 in hard cash in my pocket.

Realizing all the action from the advertisement on the Studebaker, I quickly started looking around from dealer to dealer for a Stude trade. They were so common, like shit on the sidewalks. Every one of the Champion 6 cylinder engines needed engine work. I honestly don't remember buying one that was perfect, unless the previous owner had new piston

Lemon Juice

rings installed. The salvage price ranged from $15.00 to $30.00 for them, depending on which one was not quite so bad. It was a footrace between the junkman and me to buy the car. If he was on his way to a dealer and I was there at the dealer, the dealers raised the price to me another $5.00 to $10.00. I fought like hell telling them that I would buy all they had, but I still had to give them $5.00 more than the auto graveyards. By the way, with the exception of the first one, they all belonged in the auto graveyard, and like dying elephants, they shortly found their way there.

It was a race to the dealers to see who had Studeys that they had traded. Sometimes I reached agencies that had not even been known to take them in trade and so when I came across one or two, I was able to buy them for a few dollars less.

Stopping into one dealer I wandered into a beautiful four door Commander with automatic transmission. This one didn't even have a smoking engine! That was definitely quite rare, however, it did have one drawback. It had a cracked engine block and water was spilling out profusely. I was relieved there was engine difficulties because I wouldn't know that to do with a good Studey. After all, my customers believed they were all good. How would they believe that this was better than good? A few days later, plus two pints of heavy duty block sealer, which was used on commercial boilers, the block had ceased to leak and the car was sold.

I had picked up a beautiful $15.00 Studey that was fun selling. This car smoked so much that I couldn't show it to anyone until it was a cloudy, rainy evening. It was definitely not a daytime

My First Plunge

car. I guess it was designed for formal evening use, because if this car was seen in the daytime it would attract the attention of fire departments, ambulances, arson squads and the like. It must have inspired Ian Fleming to design James Bonds' smoke screen Aston Martin. Nevertheless, in car jargon, there is an ass for every seat.

The evening came when my customer was coming to see this spotless, smokin' gem. He was in the military service and needed reliable transportation to California. He wanted to know the approximate gas mileage, which I quoted as being 'about 25 miles per gallon.' That was pretty accurate for later that evening he confirmed my calculation was correct.

I had advertised this car for $165.00 to which he responded. I felt terrible that this man had wanted the car at that price. I'm serious. I started to feel a little guilty - not a whole lot - but just a little. He wanted to take it for a test drive and listen to the engine. There was a very dense fog that hit suddenly. I quick had to move the car so that the exhaust was in the direction of the wind. I carefully placed it facing south on the crest of the hill. From there, we proceeded to take my famous "four block road test." Heading south one block then right one block and right one block and right and finally the last lap on the test drive one block and right.

We were unable to proceed the last five hundred feet because of the dense smoke which occurred from initially starting the engine. Quick, what to say? How could I get out of this one? I told him that we had to be very careful on this block because when the fog hits this area its quite dangerous and its best

Lemon Juice

to just go very slow and easy. We pulled back into the same open spot on the top of the hill. It was simply amazing that this guy loved the car. He raced up the engine and from under the hood he kept listening for knocks. He couldn't find one. One doesn't listen for bad rings, he just looks for bad rings.

Being convinced that the fog was getting more dangerous by the minute, we abandoned the car on the top of the hill and took a walk to my basement. When I asked him to give me $10.00 less, he would not do this because he didn't want to take advantage of me. I obliged by accepting his $165.00 in hard cash. It was about seven in the evening when he took the car, and it wasn't until eleven that night that I heard from him again. He was screaming mad!! He didn't seem like the nice man who had just given me the money. He called from Wildwood, New Jersey. He said, "I just got here and drove only 90 miles. I used 13 quarts of oil because the car needs a ring job!" I told him that for a mere $65.00 he could get a ring job at any service station, which was true. He then made a remark which I still today think is cute, "I'm sitting on the cheeks of my ass with all my eggs in one basket." That was a nice expression. I referred to it with compassion, thinking how tough it was to raise $65.00, I am serious. However it was tough for me to make the mortgage payments to prevent my home from being foreclosed and to help put food on the table. Him or me? I'll take me any day of the week, when it gets right down to it. He did tell me that the car did get 25 miles to the gallon, which is exactly what I told him.

My First Plunge

Jack and Libby Gordon lived only one block away from us. Libby's mother was my father's sister hence Libby was my first cousin and her son Bobby, was my first cousin once removed. They lived at 5033 Franklin Street, in the Logan section of North Philadelphia.

Jack and Libby had a tumultuous marriage. Bobby was a sweet kid who was brought up in a house of chaos. During one of their numerous breakups, Jack Gordon was living in Detroit, Michigan when Bobby was about 15 years old. Bobby went to visit his father in Detroit and one day his father, Jack, had taken him as a guest on someone's boat when tragedy struck. Bobby dove into the water not knowing that the boat was situated right above rocks. He was rushed by ambulance to the hospital with a broken spine, where he spent months in recovery. I remember driving with my cousins Josh, his wife Doris and their son Steve, through the night during a heavy downpour and storms to get to Detroit as fast as possible.

When I saw Bobby laying in a full body cast, I noticed a metal halo around his head with two bolts screwed into the area right above his ears. He never complained. I was shaken up seeing Bobby like this being paralyzed.

Month after month he went through physical therapy and eventually was transported back to his home in Logan. Through sheer will and determination, months later he was walking with an obvious limp and atrophy had set into his left arm.

He, along with some friends, took a drive to South Carolina to buy fireworks. Bobby had a total of $50 to his name, which

Lemon Juice

he spent on firecrackers with the sole intentions of selling them back home where they were illegal. After a week back home, he made over $100 and with his father's background as a used car salesman, Bobby purchased his first car with the intention of selling it. Thus, Bobby started in the used car business pretty much the same way I did. He went to the used car dealers in the area and negotiated to buy cars, no different than what I was doing. He advertised the cars in the same newspapers and was also selling them from his house. Each week he purchased another car, sometimes two, advertised them and subsequently sold them making a profit. Logan became a hotbed for kids selling cars from their homes. Raymond on Wellens Avenue was hustling cars the same way as we were. Mark Bradburg was selling cars on 11th Street from his mother's second floor apartment.

Bobby and I pretty much had the same stops and would see the same dealers. We always met sometime during the day for something to eat and would meet again in the evenings to discuss how we did individually before we became partners. We never stepped on the other's 'private stops' and were always courteous.

One day I drove over to his house to pick him up. I was seated in my car outside his house waiting for Bobby to come out. I noticed a man knocking on Bobby's front door and screaming. He kept yelling for somebody to open the door because he wanted his money back for a 1953 grey Ford sedan he had just purchased a couple hours before. That would never happen. Bobby, however remained in the house. I decided to drive around the block. All the neighbors were yelling out of their windows - but not for this guy to be quiet - instead they were yelling: *"Bobby give the man his money back - give him his money back!!"*

My cousin Bobby, who I also thought of as a good friend, and I had been selling cars from our respective homes for over one year, when we both agreed that's since we live so close to each other and work with the same car dealers, that we should do it as partners. That's how our partnership started.

At first we made our purchases together and worked jointly to get the cars cleaned and advertised for sale. But whose phone number to use? And from whose home should we sell the cars?

Bobby lived in the middle of Franklin Street one block from my house with homes nearly on top of one another. There was not enough parking spaces for the homeowners, many of which had to park a block for two away. If we were to park a few cars in close proximity to Bobby's house the neighbors would certainly complain. My home was located at an intersection affording easy access with plenty of parking, especially because there was a huge indoor parking garage directly across from my home that left room on the street for nearly 10 cars without any hassle from the neighbors.

In those days it was rare to have more than one car for each home. By using my basement, which was street-level as an 'office' the location would be ideal. I paneled and decorated the basement, so adding a desk or two was not an issue. It

Lemon Juice

was a natural 'office.' But what about the rental for this space? If the calls would be taken at my home and the customers came to my house to close the deals what should I charge? I asked Bobby if he thought $50 a month was fair. He did not agree. Instead, we agreed that I could keep the profits made for issuing tags and the transfer certificates. This was normally done at the notary public's office a mile away with the notary public keeping the profit. Instead, I made arrangements for the notary to charge us a flat fee for transferring a customer's vehicle and another flat fee for the tax service.

Since I could not issue titles from my house, I resorted to our prior practice of using cardboard from Chinese laundries. Yes, that piece of cardboard which was placed inside of pressed dress shirts was ideal to use as 'temporary tags.' As long as the Chinese laundry did not run out of cardboard, I was good to go. I issued a new cardboard tag with a person's home address and gave them a real State approved Transfer Certificate. It certainly would not pass the scrutiny of the State police officer, however, what were the chances that a customer would be stopped?

I charged whatever I thought would be acceptable. After the customer purchased the automobile from me, he was anxious to remove that temporary tag as soon as possible, fearing that perhaps we would change our mind. As always, our customers felt they were taking advantage of these teenage kids who needed money and thus were selling the car for such low prices. Therefore, I assumed that the charge for the Transfer Certificate and new tags would be acceptable even if it were a

My First Plunge

little overpriced. That year, I made $3,450 transferring tags and collecting sales tax. The papers for the actual motor vehicle work were submitted to the notary public, along with the sales tax, which I collected, so the entire transaction was processed properly for the customer.

Later that year, we were being investigated by the State police. There were complaints from car dealers who knew we were doing good business from our house and they were jealous. They made complaints to the State of Pennsylvania and tried to get us to stop selling without having the overhead of a used car lot.

I had obtained some certificates from the State for conducting business, but they did not include zoning. In order to obtain "B" tags or Used Car Dealer tags, it was required to conduct business from a Used Car lot. We worked out a deal with a notary public who was very influential with the State of Pennsylvania and we were able to get our "B" tags. The head of the Used Car Dealers Association invited, actually more like "demanded," Bobby and I attend a meeting at his car lot one evening. In the presence of the State police they questioned me about selling cars without a license. I rebuffed them by insisting that I certainly was licensed. The State trooper agreed that I had been paying the necessary fees. They then brought up the issue of zoning. I did not have the proper zoning certificates, but I figured if they didn't know I have some licenses then maybe they didn't know about the zoning licenses either. I jumped up and stated loudly, "you know fellas, you're all a pain in the ass. I run a legal, fully authorized

Lemon Juice

business from my house, which is more than I can say about you people. I pay the property taxes to the State, as the State trooper will testify.

"I handle my Motor Vehicle sales in a clear and decisive manner. I have the proper zoning or else the State would not allow me new contracts. Isn't that right trooper?"

I waited and hoped that the trooper would agree. If he did not, it would be confirming the State made a mistake by not checking. As he responded favorably to the head of the Dealers Association, I left them with the following statement: "Gentlemen, please get off my back. I'm not doing anything wrong and you know that. I'm simply trying to make a living." Bobby and I exited smiling to each other.

Not much later a State trooper appeared at my house and asked to see my titles. They were ready for an inspection which he approved. He asked me if I was conducting the transfers at my house. I informed him that I was. He then stated that I must comply with State regulations and post the prices so that customers will easily be able to see the cost for license transfer or new license plates. They must be made easily visible. I took a section of my basement wall and marked the prices for each transaction. I placed the venetian blind over it so it could be lifted in an instant for a State trooper's inspection or for the customers' edification.

I was conducting business from my house providing low-cost transportation to people who were desperately seeking bargains, many of them did get good deals, but there were

My First Plunge

some that got less than they had expected. Sometimes much less than the 'bargains' that they bargained for.

The State approved my business practices. After all, if I were to conduct business from a used car lot, the overhead would have been so extraordinary, that it would have driven me out of business in short order and adversely affected my customers. I was pleased that I found a niche business for myself and helped others in the process.

Finding parking spaces for my 'inventory' was getting more difficult. I then had a run in with Manny, the owner of the garage when I was only 12 or 13 years old, that I used to shoot marbles at using my homemade slingshot.

I had several automobiles for sale with one in front of my house on Lindley Avenue, three on the eighth Street side of my house and I parked a couple across the street on the Lindley Garage side. No one owned the parking spaces. They were strictly street parking. It was common courtesy to have one car parked in front your house and not take your neighbor's space, however across the street from my house was this large area totaling about 100 feet and no resident. So, I would park a couple cars there and that pissed off Manny. He threatened to call the zoning board if I continued to park cars there. He and his employees parked their cars there even though he had this massive storage garage, so I got pissed off too.

I tried speaking to him nicely and even gave him some occasional business to service one of my cars here and there. That did no good since he still threatened me. By threatening

Lemon Juice

me, he threatened my income. People were becoming dependent on my income since I continued my father's legacy of helping others. I had an aunt who was poor and needed a supplement to her meager income. A niece who had emotional problems and then there was paying expenses here at home.

Manny had a 1952 Buick Rivera two door hardtop in a two tome blue color. I had to teach him a lesson, I thought - and I did. One evening after enjoying a meal of hardshell crabs, I placed the trash from that meal in a brown paper bag and while no one was looking I opened the door to Manny's car and placed the bag on the floor beneath the driver seat. I guess I should have mentioned that summer was particularly hot that year and the heat within any automobile with the windows up would have been stifling.

Manny lived only two blocks away and for some unknown reason had not used his car for a few days. It would not have made any difference if he used the car the following day. The damage was done. When Manny eventually opened up the door to his Buick he almost passed out. The air was gone. No one could live for more than a couple minutes inhaling the fumes that were given off. He was incredibly upset and probably figured out what had happened. No one could stand near the automobile or even walk by without inhaling those horrible, putrid fumes. Even though he left the windows down in the car for a few days and had the interior removed and scrubbed, he could not get rid of the smell. A tow truck came and removed the car forever to the confines of an automobile graveyard. The next time I saw Manny, I looked at him and

My First Plunge

without hesitation said: "I guess you must have pissed off somebody," and walked away. From that day forward I had all the parking spaces that I needed.

I took up all the parking spaces around my house and a few across the street filled with new inventory. I wanted to do something special to bring customers in, as I was concerned with the traffic on 8th Street interfering with a potential sale. I purchased a theater spotlight that had a rotating wheel with alternating colors. I don't remember where I was able to find the pair of road block barriers that I used to block off the street. The problem was neighbors would have to go all the way around the block and come into their rear driveways in order to gain access to their homes. There were numerous cars for sale, lights flashing and the road blocked off. As soon as this was all set up the police arrived insisting that I remove the barriers. I told them it's just for a couple hours that evening and I needed it for business. I handed each police officer $3 and told them that by 9:30pm I would remove the barriers, which I did.

With Bobby and I selling cars from my house, the newspapers were under pressure from the local automobile dealers association to make certain that my advertisements stated "Dealer." The newspapers caved in because they did not want to lose very profitable advertising. We started a new account with the newspapers: "GORLUS" and "EPIS." No one had any idea what that meant, nor did we. It was just to throw off the automobile dealers that were constantly tracking the business that I was generating from my home.

Lemon Juice

I had signs made up in cardboard 24 inches by 18 inches: GORLUS. I told Bobby I needed a ladder, a hammer and some sheetrock nails. From Fifth Street and Roosevelt Boulevard (US 1) to Broad Street (3/4 of a mile away), I nailed the GORLUS signs to trees on both sides of the highway.

Roosevelt Boulevard was a very attractive area that was part of the Fairmount Park System. Trees abounded on the boulevard's grassy areas. After about two dozen signs were installed, a Fairmount Park Guard police car pulled right up to me. "What are you doing?" he asked. I looked at him and said that I am only following instructions to place signs on the boulevard welcoming GORLUS the famous gorilla, who is going to be part of the circus. The guard had no idea what I was talking about. Neither did I. Now, when customers called, I would instruct them to simply follow the signs for "GORLUS," since underneath the sign I had also nailed directional arrows leading the way to my street. If nothing else, at least I was inventive.

Sales from my home were now extremely active with people constantly looking for bargains, however I was running into one problem. I was purchasing the cars at auction on Wednesdays at NADE and by 2 o'clock that same day I was phoning in my classified advertisements to our local newspapers for that evening's publication. The response was tremendous, but I needed the motor vehicle titles. Customers were complaining that they had made their purchase but had not yet received the titles nor the metal permanent license plates. They would constantly call me and the notary public that handled the

My First Plunge

transaction. I told them the papers were being processed however, the Pennsylvania Department of Motor Vehicles was slow with the paperwork. That was the truth, however it was compounded by the fact that the State sometimes took two or perhaps even three weeks processing the titles into my name and then two or three weeks into my customers names. The quicker that I could get the titles, the less hassle after the sale.

The notary public who handled the motor vehicle transactions was paid additional money for 24 hour service, but in due course they were taking all too long. In talking with one car dealer, I was informed that you could get New Jersey titles in your name using a Pennsylvania address. This was interesting because New Jersey Motor Vehicle was unlike Pennsylvania. You could fill out the proper forms at one of dozens of state licensed motor vehicle offices and the titles would be processed immediately. So that's what I did. For weeks after making purchases at National Auto Dealers Exchange auction, I immediately placed the title into my name at the closest NJ motor vehicle agency. After a few weeks of doing this successfully, I was informed by the agent at the NJ DMV that they would no longer process titles in my name because the State law in New Jersey declared that any person who had 12 vehicles titled in their name in one year was considered a "car dealer."

It was simple at first. I went to other motor vehicle agencies in different areas, however it wasn't too long until they realized what I was doing and shut me off. I remembered a conversation about a large new car distributor. They used a white pages

Lemon Juice

telephone directory to come up with various names and addresses. They were paid a larger commission if they did not receive any trade-ins so to eliminate the appearance of the trade-in, they got titles in various peoples names and just assigned it to their company or sold them to other dealers. If a large distributor could do this, why couldn't I?

I started using the telephone directory for names and addresses and received cooperation from the agencies for quite a while. When they saw that we were getting titles in different names they were confused so we decided to have other people going into the offices pretending that it was their title. Someone, somewhere had a title in their name for a day or two. They never realized it. It didn't hurt anyone. It was simply a matter of convenience. Then I figured that it was really simple to do so I made up names and addresses instead of using the directory.

Chapter Five

Jail

I was at NADE when I heard my name being paged over the loudspeaker directing me to come to the manager's office. I was introduced to a gentleman in a gray suit. I reached out to shake his hand. He reached out with handcuffs and told me I was under arrest for 'title fraud.' I explained to him what I was doing and why. He was very understanding. It didn't make any difference since I was under arrest and the next thing was to post bail. I then asked him how much bail was. He told me for this case it would be $5,000. I then asked him to come with me while I checked with some friends of mine to get the cash. He said he would release me and when I got the money together to meet him in the front office of the building.

I quickly found my partner Bobby and told my brother Wes who was also at the auction. Wesley told me to get the hell out of there as soon as possible because he didn't believe that cop. I walked out the back of the auction lot as my brother made a dash for his car. He was on the other side of the fence and both Bobby and I had to hop over. That wasn't too easy

Lemon Juice

for two slightly overweight people. I pushed on Bobby's ass as he tried to get over the fence. On the other side of the fence was Wes pulling on Bobby's arms. Finally, we moved this mass of ass over the fence. I got over on my own power and we left in the waiting 'escape' vehicle.

"Let's take the Burlington Bristol Bridge," my brother Wes said, because it was the closest to the Pennsylvania border. My heart was pounding faster and faster with adrenaline pumping like mad. Finally, we made it into the Philadelphia area. Once on our home turf we organized ourselves, or so we thought. Two teenage kids in such a mess, compounded by the fact that now we were escaped 'felons' - of sorts.

We called the State trooper and apologized. He told us that it did not bother him and that he recommended we turn ourselves in as soon as possible. We met him personally and he advised us that since we admitted what we did and no harm was done, that we shouldn't even spend the money for a lawyer as we should just plead "Nolo contendere." [*No contest*]. We got fucked! One of the dumbest things that I've ever done. We found ourselves appearing in the Camden County Courthouse in front of a judge. Bobby and I were dressed neatly. I was wearing a black three-piece suit carrying an umbrella as it was a dismal, rainy day.

"Robert H. Gordon," the court bailiff shouted. Bobby stood up and I walked with him and approached the bench. The judge asked "Are you Robert H. Gordon?" "I am," Bobby replied. "And how do you plead?" "Nolo contendere," replied Bobby.

Jail

The judge looked at me and said "You had better arrange bail for your client, counselor. Then Bobby was escorted by a guard to the rear of the courtroom where he was placed in a holding tank. "Eugene H. Epstein? Eugene H. Epstein? Eugene H. Epstein?" I kept walking as the bailiff repeatedly called my name.

Now Bobby was sitting there on a metal cot wondering what to do. He couldn't do a damn thing sitting there, but I could. I told him that I would work on something immediately. He looked at me like a frightened soul. "I'm starving," he said. I told him that while I would be trying to figure out what to do I would be sure to bring him something to eat.

I left the courtroom as they were still calling my name. Down one street and up another looking for a bail bondsman. They were all around like prostitutes peering out some windows looking for business. The prices that were quoted to me to post bail were outrageous. I went to speak with one bondsman who was in an office shared with an assemblyman. He wanted $7,000 in cash to post bail. I already got fucked once this day and wasn't going for another.

Finally, I found the lesser of many thieves who would charge us 10% of the $5,000 bail, which came to $500 in cash for each of us. The bail bondsman would make the arrangements and meet us at the courthouse within a half-hour. I stopped at a luncheonette for a hoagie for each of us along with two lemon Tastykake pies and two bags of Wise Potato Chips. "Please give this to my partner," I told the guard. "And let me in there with him."

Lemon Juice

The guard told me that I was not permitted inside the holding tank; that it was only for persons being held pending sentencing or bail. I told him that I was Eugene H. Epstein and within moments I was sharing the same cell with my partner, Bobby, who was chomping away on the fattest Hoagie I could find.

Thirty minutes passed, which seemed more like a day... no bondsman in sight. Now the guards were opening the cell and I felt a short-lived relief. They were not releasing us but instead taking us up the elevator directly to the prison upstairs. No bail. We were going straight to jail!! Oh shit. Another scary experience. We stood all the while the prison receptionist asked us for information. I told him that we were waiting for the bail bondsman, who would show up any second.

After pleading with him to let us remain seated where we were, he told us it was too late. Prisoners still wore gray stripped uniforms and he instructed another guard to take us to a cell. "Wait!" cried the bondsman as he hurriedly approached. "They are my clients and I have the papers for their release." I was never so glad to see someone as I was just then. Bobby is the boss and he made a deal for 6%. Free at last! Free at last!!

The bondman touted us to some politicians in the area. We spoke to several of them. They were even bigger thieves than the bondmen were. Each wanted cash in hand with no guarantees. One said for $5,000 he could guarantee that we wouldn't go to jail. However, we would still have a criminal record.

Jail

I called my brother Wes and that was all that was needed. He mentioned a judge in Burlington New Jersey and then recommended a brilliant criminal lawyer. Ben Asbell was a former prosecutor for the State for nine years and was highly respected. We told him everything that had transpired and he told us that his representation would be a flat fee of $500. When he heard our testimony and realized there was no criminal intent and no one suffered a monetary loss, he informed the judge and our case was dismissed and this time we were really free. Thank God!!

Chapter Six

Back to Business

Both Bobby and I had mutually agreed to be gentlemen respecting each other's stops at car dealers to make our purchases. If I had been purchasing cars from a particular new car dealer Bobby would not venture there to give me competition and vice versa. This was fine except when it came to one dealer that we both frequented, Koelle-Greenwood Ford in the Germantown section of Philadelphia. Bobby would stop there and so would I. Often we would discuss their inventory of used cars that they had just traded.

One evening Bobby and another friend Raymond, who was also selling automobiles from his house just two blocks away, were talking about cars they had purchased that day. I had asked them about a few cars at Koelle-Greenwood Ford. They responded that they were not going to buy the cars they had because in their opinion the prices were too high. I then felt that I would try to make a deal with the owner's son at the Ford dealership.

Back to Business

The following morning I drove there and was at the used car lot by 8:30 that morning. I had to get the assistance from the porter to help me get these "junkers" started because many had dead batteries. I don't know how many people were driving them the weeks and days before, as it seemed as though they probably had only enough strength to make it to the new car dealers to be traded-in and then collapsed. Maybe it was like an elephant finding strength to travel the untold miles to reach their ancestral burial grounds(?) But there they lay.

Exhausted batteries with not enough power to turn the engine. Oil pouring out of one like an elephant oozing blood after poachers shot them without mercy. Well, here I was with a set of hotshot cables in hand looking like a doctor administering emergency shock treatments, trying to bring back the dead.

I had successfully started and road tested five cars. In my mind, I decided how much I wanted to pay and the prices that I would get for them. I started at 9:30am, to deal with the owner's son Robert. After a marathon of negotiations, it was nearly 2pm until we agreed on the prices. It was still in the range that I originally decided so I signed the paperwork at his desk and wrote out my check. Immediately, I designed five advertisements for these cars to be placed in the Philadelphia Inquirer for that evenings newspaper. As long as the advertisements were called in by 3pm they would make that evening's early edition.

Lemon Juice

I took my car home which was about 5 miles and grabbed a couple of neighborhood kids that had driver's licenses. I gave them $1.00 each for driving the cars to my home. They would have done this for nothing, simply for the fun of driving a car. By 4pm the cars were at my house. At this point, they needed a mass cleanup. All cars needed a severe compounding and waxing but this was time-consuming and expensive. I expected customers to be calling and arriving later in the evening so the cars had to be ready.

I mixed up a lot of oil and varnish and used a clean towel to wipe down some of the cars exterior finishes. This combination made the exterior shine like a new paint job but would rapidly transition to a milky finish in a couple of days.

One of my purchases was a very nice 1951 Chevrolet with 'Powerglide' transmission. This car's transmission leaked so badly that it would only hold fluid for a few minutes. Therefore, I carefully swept off the leaves on the street and placed a mound of them in one area where I parked the Chevy on top of the leaves. Good! That's one car ready to go.

About 75 feet away there was a parking space in front of the Schwartzman's house. I placed the 1952 Plymouth convertible there. The car was very nice looking but had a weak battery and a weak engine. When it warmed up there was a noticeable engine-rod bearing knock. Not a severe one, nor one that could not be easily repaired, but one that should be saved from the dreaded burial grounds of the auto graveyards.

Back to Business

Across the street I placed a very lonely looking 1950 Dodge Wayfarer coupe. It was called a 'businessman coupe' for having a platform over the seat for salesmen to store items to sell. The car ran well. Obviously, it had a dead battery but it's still ran well. It had a beautiful finish which would last up to 48 hours then would rapidly decay. It would however provide good transportation.

In my driveway, which separated our house from the Schwartzman's house, I placed an enormous 1950 Buick Super sedan. All the actors were in their place awaiting the audience to arrive. The calls came deluging in. One, two, five, ten! Oh my God! I received nearly **40** calls and everyone wanted to come right away!! Oh shit!

It seemed as if they came in droves. The first to arrive was a young doctor who was a resident at a Center City Philly hospital. He wanted to see the 1950s Buick Super sedan which was parked in my driveway. That was about 7:30pm. As I was showing him the beneficial features of the Buick, I noticed several people walking around in front of my house. I questioned if I could help them. They ALL wanted to see the 1951 Chevy. I pointed to the car, which was only about 50 feet away and showed it to six people at once. They were all interested in it so I suggested taking it for a test drive. There was no sense in taking them one at a time, so I told all of them to squeeze in. This, they did! They literally all squeezed into the four-door Chevy, which immediately became a seven passenger automobile, albeit one where if one person farted, everybody would choke.

Lemon Juice

I chauffeured the group of seven including myself around the block. It was a simple city square block and in minutes we were back. It was good that there was so much interest in the car since it would have been difficult to drive the car much more than the four square blocks because the car was leaving a trail of transmission fluid behind.

As I returned with the group of potential customers, I asked who wanted to buy the automobile? Requesting a show of hands, four potential buyers' hands were elevated. I asked the interested parties if they could leave a deposit and then there was a show of two hands lifted as high as the headliner in the automobile so that I could easily see who was left that were still interested. Then, I asked who had the entire $285 and one hand was raised. "You sir, are the lucky buyer!" I stated and within minutes, the new owner was driving off smiling as the car disappeared into the night, proudly showing off the temporary cardboard license plate, which I affixed to the car.

By the time this transaction was completed there were two young men looking at the '52 Plymouth convertible. One was hearing impaired and the other was his close friend. It was a clean car that was in excellent condition with the exception of the engine bearing noise. They wanted time to listen to the engine thoroughly through their fingertips feeling for vibrations. While they were feeling the automobile, I showed another revival in 1950 Dodge 'business coupe.' One drive around the block was all that car needed. I gave the customer a $1 allowance for the missing gasoline filler cap. A $155 later,

Back to Business

I saw the proud new owner driving the car away and disappear over the horizon.

The hearing impaired customer and his friend were still around and surprised me by saying the car is fine - but needed some engine work - which they could perform themselves! They handed me $285 and another shirt cardboard was applied to the rear of the vehicle for a temporary license plate and off into the setting sun for them.

I was amazed at the ability of the hearing impaired person to feel the sensitivity of the engine knock through his fingertips. I was glad that he knew what was wrong and was able to repair it. No matter what price I was selling my cars for, they were still so much less than retail that the customer would have wiggle room to make repairs wherever necessary. Once the car was repaired it was worth double the price that I sold it for, so they actually got a good buy.

Between taking people for test drives, running into the house to answer phones and directing people to my house, taking money, issuing temporary registrations, so that the cars could be removed immediately from my property to make room for the next day's purchases, I was bushed!

I called Bobby at his house and told him to get Raymond and come over. I wanted to treat them to a late night out. They arrived about 15 minutes later and I told him that I sold out — but did I?

Lemon Juice

There was a noise which came from the rear of my house. Oh no! I forgot about that doctor. After two hours of waiting for me, he wanted to know if he could buy the Buick. Buicks were traditionally sold to people who wanted a comfortable, large car with a plush interior.

Surprisingly, I had only one call for that car and it was from him. I apologized for keeping him so long. Honestly, where the car was parked and had only this one customer, I paid scant attention to this vehicle, while everyone else wanted to purchase immediately.

I gave him a receipt for his money and got the car running. He completed the picture of a closeout sale that was very prosperous for me. The entire day's transaction netted $700 in profits! This was considered an enormous sum in those days. I could see my future carved out in front of me - this is what I was meant to do. I just hoped the Chinese laundry didn't run out of cardboard.

As a buyer of used automobiles for my business, it was not unusual for me to carry a great deal of cash. Most times the amounts I carried on a daily basis consisted of several thousands dollars in denominations of one hundred dollar bills.

I used to carry the cash in my left front pants pocket to make it easily accessible to me. Years later, when I was having my clothes custom designed, I'd have my shirts made with a buttoned pocket on my left front to hold additional cash in the event that I was robbed or for emergency purposes.

Back to Business

One day I received a telephone call from a woman at a dry cleaning establishment in North Philadelphia. "Mr. Epstein, did you leave any money in your pants pocket?" The woman asked. "I certainly did." I replied. I had no idea if there was a dollar in there or $1,500, since I was dealing in cash payments for automobiles. At 18 years of age, I was making so much money that I kept large sums on me in order to convince auto dealers that I was a serious buyer, especially if they did not know me personally. Why take a chance that some kid is giving you a check that may not be good?

I drove to the dry cleaners on Old York Road to pick up whatever of my cash was there. The woman showed me my pants and asked if they were mine - they were. She then told me there was $900 in my left front pocket. In today's dollars that $900 in 1958 would be equivalent to about $10,000 - a hefty sum by anyone's standards. The funny thing is, I did not miss that money. I wasn't looking around the house concerned 'where is my $900?'

She didn't have to contact me about the money; she could have kept it all for herself and run off to live the high life in the South of France for the rest of her life and I probably never would have known the difference. But she called right away to let me know she found my money in my pants pocket because she was a woman with high moral ethics.

I was so taken by her integrity, that I gave her $100 as my way of thanking her for her kindness and honesty. I also gave her a big, grateful hug! She later told me she made $36 a week for working there and the $100 gratuity meant the world to her.

Lemon Juice

As a kid I never slept much. My mother used to tell stories how she would get up for work very early and would always go check to see that I was sleeping since I had chronic sinusitis and numerous allergies that necessitated four injections in each arm twice weekly.

At 6 o'clock in the morning my mom opened the bedroom door and I was nowhere to be found. She knew that I came home that evening and went to bed, but couldn't figure out where I was.

Every morning my mother would spend a half-hour 'doing herself up' until she was satisfied that she was impeccable, however this particular morning she was concerned. She checked downstairs and then decided to go to the basement where my office was located, then being relieved to see that the office door was open. She stuck her head outside and saw that there was approximately 4 inch of snow accumulation from the night before. She was reassured seeing the hood open on one of my cars and I was laying underneath in the snow on my back changing the oil. I was diligent in taking care of my cars hoping for a quick sale.

Not every car was a quick purchase, clean up, advertise and sale. But some were. One such car sale started with a late night phone call from a man with a heavy Southern accent responding to my advertisement for a '51 Studebaker, as usual.

He was an Army colonel and told me he just flew in from Germany where he had been stationed and wanted to buy the car I was advertising for sale. He was going to figure out how he could get from the airport to my home in Logan. The problem was that he wanted to come out that night and it was already 10:30pm when I spoke with him. I requested that he come at 7 o'clock in the morning but he insisted that he had the cash in hand and wanted to be on the road heading to Cheyenne, Wyoming that night.

I told the colonel to come on to my address and that I would wait for him. It was after midnight when he finally arrived, wearing a tall cowboy hat and cowboy boots. He looked at the car and seemed satisfied. I insisted that he take it for a drive before purchasing it. Not only that but he could only see the car by light of the half-moon out that night. He had the money in his hand and tried to give it to me, but I told him I would not take it unless he was satisfied with the car after test driving it.

Because he was a colonel in the Army, I did not take him for the test drive but told him to get behind the wheel and that <u>he</u> should take it for drive. He handled the car without any problems through all the gears and took it up a hill where he brought the car to a stop. *"You've got a mighty fine car there,"* he said with his southern drawl. *"<u>Now</u> will you take my money?"*

I think I felt bad about selling one of my Studebakers, which needed new rings, to a serviceman, but I graciously agreed to make the sale and accepted his money. I wished him good luck as he drove off into the sunset with his new purchase and the cardboard license plate from the Chinese laundry attached to the back with the words: *"Cheyenne or bust"* handwritten on the cardboard plate.

Lemon Juice

Two days later the Army colonel called to thank me. That was the first time anyone went to the trouble of ever calling me back without it being a complaint.

At home, I had a beautiful 1956 Mercury convertible for sale. It was salmon in color with cream to make a handsome two tone combination. I was able to buy it at an extraordinarily reasonable price because the transmission was erratic. Sometimes it would work fine while other times the transmission would either slip through gears or shake. It was a toss-up anytime you drove it which mood it was in. I had the car priced very reasonably so anyone purchasing it could certainly afford to get the transmission fixed, that is, if they knew this repair was needed.

A man in his 50s and his wife came to buy the car as a surprise for their son. The man looked at the car with his wife and he said okay. He purchased the car without even taking it for a test drive; not even starting the engine! His wife begged him "Please don't buy it. He's only a kid." At that time I wasn't sure if she was referring to their son or to me when she said "he's only a kid," however within 48 hours I came to a total realization of who I sold the car to.

I received a call from the new purchaser a day after he had purchased the car and brought it home. "The transmission is shot in this car," he said somewhat calmly. "I bought this for my son who is dying of bladder cancer." I didn't know what to say. I felt bad but I did sell the car 'as is' and it was cheap. His wife was screaming in the background. "I begged you not buy the car from that kid. He's so young. Please leave him alone." He told her that he will take care of this matter himself. I thought that meant that he was going to fix the transmission himself. How wrong I was. About 15 minutes after that telephone call I received yet another call, but this time from the wife. She explained that her husband was an electrician who wired illegal gambling joints for the mob, to which he belonged. I was not really happy with our conversation - to say the least. I told her that I would gladly refund his money that I had no idea that their son was so gravely ill. A few minutes later I received a call that their son liked the car and the father did not want to bring it back. I then told him that I would be glad to fix the transmission and get a rebuilt one for him, providing he could get the car to the transmission shop. He agreed.

I asked the manager at the transmission shop off of Old York Road to road test the Mercury convertible and let me know if anything else needed attention. He told me the radio was not working but a shop that he does business with could repair it. Also, the zipper for the rear convertible window was broken. I authorized the repair and replacement of the rear window and the radio as well.

A couple of days later the car was finished and my customer picked it up. He saw the bill was almost as much as I had sold the car for and then told me that he owed me one major favor in life. The 'favor' he explained would be the ultimate one without mentioning anything else. I put his name and phone number on a business card and put it in the back of my wallet never knowing if I would ever have to use that 'ultimate' favor.

Lemon Juice

Nearly a year went by and I never thought anything about that particular sale until an incident happened at NADE, the automobile auction in Bordentown.

I had been the top bidder on a school bus that was only a few hundred dollars. The dealer who sold the school bus was a fellow named Larry. He used to sell 30 cars a week at the Bordentown auction. I took the bus for a mechanical test drive and found that the seller misrepresented its condition. I filled out the paperwork to bring the vehicle to what was termed the 'arbitration' adjustment where representatives of the auction house would have their in-house mechanics road test it to either confirm or refute my complaint.

Outside in the vast parking lot was the bus after being checked by the auction house's mechanics. The seller, who stood at least a head taller than me, came up to me pissed off knowing that the problems with the bus were confirmed by the mechanics, which he never divulged. Before I had anything to say, he threw a left-hand punch to the side of my jaw. It dropped me to the ground in a flash. Laying flat on the ground he was on top of me like a wrestler, a <u>big</u> wrestler. A few people pulled him off of me and I, with a bloody nose, straightened myself out and went inside to make a phone call.

The telephone room look like a bookie joint, not that I've ever been in one, but just what I've seen in movies. There were over a dozen pay phones on the walls and several dealers with either cigarettes or cigars dangling from their mouths using the phones. I picked up one of the phones and looked for some change. Finding that I had none, I asked a couple guys next to me for some coins. It was a long distance phone call to Pennsylvania and my prior customer answered. I told him exactly what had happened and he asked me to get as much information as I could about the man who punched me from his full name to a home address, business address and what days he attended the Bordentown auction.

I didn't understand at the time what I was asking for. I'm not sure the 'electrician' and I were on the same page. I was just damned mad that I had been sucker-punched in the face and beaten up while I was down on the ground. I just wanted to 'get even,' maybe have Larry beaten up too in retaliation. The gravity of the situation didn't dawn on me until after I had the conversation with my customer. He said "Don't worry. It'll be taken care of within one week." He also said that if it has to be in New Jersey he would have to sub out "the job," since he only operated in Pennsylvania. I was trembling, not certain if it was from the shock of being punched in the jaw and beaten, or because I just spoke to a 'hitman' or who I thought was a hitman. I wasn't even sure if there was some miscommunication between us.

Within what seemed to be just 15 minutes, a couple of very large New Jersey State troopers confronted me. They told me that they knew I just placed a call to have the dealer that owned the bus — killed. There is no way that I would have ordered such a thing to be done, nor for the troopers to have known. However, one of the dealers that was on the phone, who gave me the change to make the phone call, worked for Larry. He must have overheard my conversation and assumed

I was ordering a 'hit' on Larry. There was nothing that the State troopers could do from a hearsay phone call and I knew that they certainly did not have the pay phones tapped. I adamantly denied what they were accusing me of doing, because in my mind, I hadn't done anything, but they put me on notice by warning me that they were interested in Larry's safety and well-being.

The next day when Larry heard about the phone call, he got scared and called to apologize to me. I told him to go fuck himself. "I'm sorry. What can I do?" He asked. I told him for the next four weekly auctions he is not to bring one automobile to the auction, which was his livelihood for turning used cars into cash. He begged me to let him miss just one auction since anymore would kill him financially. I laughed and smugly replied: "Which way do you want it? Your cash or your life?" Ordinarily, that might have seemed like an empty threat from a young kid - but it was a kid who appeared to have a hitman at his disposal. Now that threat packed lethal weight.

When I rolled all this around in my mind, I realized I made a terrible mistake. I made my next phone call from another pay phone purposely near my home. It was to the purchaser of my Mercury convertible. I told him I didn't want Larry to be beaten up, or any harm to come to him; to just drop the whole thing. It would bother me too much knowing this fight escalated so far. He was pissed off to say the least. He told me that he already authorized someone in Burlington County that was going to take care of the 'matter' this week and that it was embarrassing to him to have to cancel it. He did cancel "the

Back to Business

job" but admonished me to "Throw away my phone number. Never call me again. Forget my name." Honestly, to this day I forgot his name.

Larry abstained from attending the auction for the next four weeks. When I saw him on the fifth week, he came over to me, put his arm around my shoulders and once again said "I am truly sorry." And this time I think he sincerely meant it.

On a trip to Acapulco, Mexico a few years later, we stayed at the beautiful El Conquistador Hotel situated on the crest of a mountain. I was not a gambler so there was little for me to do. I purchased a book about the writings of Edgar Cayce, a world famous metaphysician, which changed my life. In the book, it said that hatred is a cancer which only affects the person holding the hatred. The person that caused your anger is unaffected. The person that holds anger and hatred destroys themselves from within. From that day forward, I have forgiven people and never used the word "hatred" again.

When back home, to relieve the stress, Bobby, Ray and I headed out to get some late evening eating which we did quite often. On the way to the restaurant, Ray wanted to get laid, so did Bobby. I did go along and offered to treat. Ray said "Let's go to Paula the whore." Ray knew them all. He drove us near Temple University in this two-toned Chrysler Imperial. The neighborhood was in the heart of North Philadelphia; mostly a seedy neighborhood at the time. We were crazy - but what else was new?

Lemon Juice

It was a laborious climb to the third floor apartment which the prostitute occupied. Knocking on her door got looks from other apartments. "Let's get out of here," I said, but neither would listen. They were all charged up and ready to go. Paula opened the door. What I saw was nauseating. An old woman, very haggard with red dyed hair was greeting her dear friend, Ray. "Come on fellas, let's get out here," but it didn't work. Ray decided that since he told us about her that he should at least go first. As far as I was concerned he could go first, second and last, as long as we could get out of that neighborhood - and fast.

He was escorted to the rear bedroom where he and Paula went at it. A few minutes later Bobby had his turn. This was too much. No way was I going to go near that whore. I would not even let her even grab my hand. Ray was ready to walk down the stairs to leave and I yelled to Bobby that I was not going to wait any longer so he had better hurry. Ray and I ran down the steps and headed for the car. Once we were inside the car, we locked ourselves in. Then I leaned on the horn. Lights in the entire area were being turned on to see what was happening. I looked towards the stairs and heard Bobby yelling "Fellas, wait! Just wait! Don't leave me here!! She doesn't want me to leave. She is in love with me. Please wait… Please wait…" Bobby had his shoes and socks in his hand and nearly tripped hobbling down those stairs.

One of Bobby's previous salesman was Harmon Wasserman, known to all his friends and family as "Herkie" who sold cars from his home on a commission basis for Bobby.

Back to Business

Herkie's parents had emigrated from Russia and were kind and generous souls. When Herkie was old enough to drive, they wanted to buy him a car, but not knowing much about cars or the process, they asked Herkie to see if I could help them out, knowing that I was in the car business.

Herkie had seen a magnificent turquoise and white 1958 Ford Fairlane 500 convertible at Koelle Greenwood Ford. He fell in love with the automobile upon first sight - and I believe the feeling was mutual. Herkie and the car couldn't take their respective eyes/headlights off of one another. He was smitten with that car and the dealer was amenable to selling the Fairlane to them at a discounted price as a courtesy to me, since I was purchasing cars from them for resale.

I drove Herkie and his mother to the Ford dealership in Germantown. Once we arrived and were standing in the showroom, Mrs. Wasserman pulled me aside and with her deep Russian accent said *"Make sure Herkie get new tires."* She must have thought the dealer might sell them a new car with used tires. In Russia, if you were fortunate enough to buy a 'new' car, it was a dilapidated used hooptie and usually came with only three tires - and they were worn down to the nub. The fourth tire? Well, that was your problem.

So her interest in making sure her son received the top of the line vehicle with associated accouterments such as 'new' tires was understandable. Everyone went home happy that day, including the car, for it now had a loving home - and four new tires.

Lemon Juice

In 1957 I graduated from Olney High School with narrowly passing grades and went to Temple University with a Senatorial scholarship. Oh, I purchased the scholarship from my John Hancock insurance agent, who back in 1957 was selling scholarships for $200 a semester. I paid our insurance agent the money, a portion of which supposedly went to a senator. My interest was in law and at that time I was thinking of someday being a prosecutor.

I attended classes which I had scheduled from 8 o'clock in the morning to no later than 1pm. I wanted to get out of school as early as I could so I could still get to my various new car dealer's facilities to see if they traded something that I could use.

Time was very important to me and when I drove from my home in Logan to Broad Street and Montgomery Avenue where my classes were located, I needed to find in-and-out parking. Less than a half block from my classes was a school parking lot for students, which cost either 25¢ or 50¢ a day. I tried parking there one day and walked to class while waiting for traffic to ease for me to cross safely.

I noticed the spot right in front of the doorway to the building was reserved for the Dean of the university. Not only was it reserved for the Dean, but there was a large City sign that prohibited parking at *anytime* other than in an allocated parking space. I found out that anyone who parked in the Dean's space, even for a short period of time, wound up almost immediately with a parking ticket.

Back to Business

My first class was uneventful. It was a business finance class taught by Dr. Jackendorf. I remember seeing him wearing a blue suit the first day of class and also saw him weeks later. Everybody who showed up in class wound up getting a grade of "B." I thought, 'what was the sense of going to class?'

One of my other classes was in Economics. The professor was a consultant for the United States government whose expertise was in economics. The only thing that sticks in my mind to this day is that he was giving the class his theory on economics and spoke about how in some cultures, pigs' eyes have value. This was not for me either.

The one class I thoroughly enjoyed was pre-law. The professor was Dr. Tommy Roberts. With over two dozen students in the class, Dr. Roberts called me out in front of the entire class one day: "Epstein! You are the only one here asking questions. All of your questions and responses seem interesting and the rest of the class should be paying rapt attention!" Pre-law was the only subject that kept me interested enough to keep me in school, even with two-thirds of that semester behind me.

After class one day, Tommy came over to me and said "Epstein, you are going to be a great lawyer one day and I'm going to recommend you after graduation to one of the top law firms in Philadelphia. Instead of making $9,000 a year, as most graduating students do, I'm sure you'll get a job that pays $13,000 a year to start at a top law firm!"

I put my arm around Tommy's back and guided him towards the Broad Street side of the classroom, then I asked Tommy

Lemon Juice

to look down at the Dean's parking space. I asked him to tell me what he saw. "It looks like a new Chrysler Imperial," he responded. I told him that is **my** car and everyday I have been parking in the Dean's parking space getting a $3.00 ticket. I told him my time was too valuable to look for parking close to the university when for a mere $3.00 a day, I could park in the Dean's parking space right by the entrance!

Then, I explained to Tommy that I am making $20,000 a year selling used cars after he told me it will take me several more years to be able to make $13,000 once I graduated and worked for a top notch law firm. I gave him a big hug because I really did like this professor so much. I learned a great deal from him. I then handed him all of my books and asked him to give them to someone who needed them, as this was my last day at school.

Chapter Seven

Marlene and Matilda

I met Marlene in 1955. Marlene Bernice Perez lived in a large home at 5114 North 11th Street in Logan, only three streets from my home. One day Bobby and I went to a party that she had (more like several friends getting together) in her basement. We went to the rear entrance of her house and knocked on the door. Someone from inside asked who I was and what I wanted. I said that 'I am here for the party' (which I was crashing since neither of us had an invitation). "Get that Epstein kid out of here," came a voice from the basement. That was the loudest sound I would ever hear from Marlene. We never made it inside the house to the party, so Bobby and I left.

Shortly after, I had a couple of dates with her girlfriend, Shirley, who visited Marlene often where I would pick her up. A couple of dates later with Shirley, Marlene was now speaking to me and I was so glad, that I stopped dating Shirley and asked Marlene out. That started our 60 plus year love story. Marlene would walk from her home on 11th Street to my home on 8th

Lemon Juice

Street and from there we would walk hand-in-hand to Olney High School which we both attended.

When I had a car (which was often), our dates would be going to various local car dealers to see the cars that they were about to trade that evening. One of my favorite spots was John B. White Ford, which was located on the 4900 block of North Broad Street. The agency was run by a father and son. The father Roy Chapman Sr., ran the new car sales and his son Roy Chapman Jr. (Chappy) was the used car manager who decades later would become the world renown owner of the racehorse "Smarty Jones." Both Sr and Jr always had cigarettes hanging from their mouths. They were pleasant and I guess that they admired a 16 year old kid doing business with them as their peers.

In the mornings prior to school, I would drive by and pick up Marlene and return to their dealership's used car lot to see if they made deals on the cars from the previous night. Both were there early and I would negotiate with Chappy Jr., as quickly as possible and pay for my purchase, then head to school.

At the 11 o'clock break I would phone in my advertisement(s) for that evening. We did this as a routine stopping at JB White then a bit north on Broad Street to W.T. Jones Chrysler-Plymouth. From their used car manager to the owners, we had a great relationship. If I didn't stop by one day and they traded a car that they thought I would want, they actually called me and held the car before wholesaling it to other dealers to give me first crack at them.

Marlene and Matilda

After several dates with Marlene, I introduced her to my mother, Matilda, who fell in love with her immediately! Why not? Marlene was and is to this day, over 60 years later, the most wonderful, caring and lovable person in the world. My mother, Tillie (or Billie as she loved to be called), had always remarked that Marlene was the daughter she didn't have to go through the pains of childbirth to have.

Now, a few years went by and Marlene and I were walking the boardwalk in Ventnor, New Jersey. My brother Mickey and his wife, Nancy, were walking on the boardwalk toward us with some friends that we hadn't seen in a while. Mickey introduced us: "This is my brother Gene and this is Marlene his…..his….er fiancée." I looked at Marlene and said "I guess that we just got engaged…"

We married in 1960 when she was 19 and I was 21 years of age. We have two children, Ellen and Robert. Having a wife and family was further incentive to provide for them. And I made it my business to do exactly that. Regrettably though, our marriage got off to a rocky start.

The morning following our marriage, both Marlene and I headed to Miami Beach for a two week honeymoon. We stayed at the fabulous Fontainebleau Hotel. At home, was my mother and Pierre our incredibly intelligent French poodle, which was my engagement present to Marlene. I could have purchased a magnificent diamond ring for Marlene, since I was doing very well financially, however that did not impress Marlene. She wanted a doggie.

Lemon Juice

The year before, I went to a pet shop in Philadelphia to purchase a dog. I had no idea what to look for. There, I saw two black poodle puppies. One in a cage next to the other. The poodle on the left was $85 and the other was $135. I asked the proprietor what the difference in cost was because to me, they both looked the same. The owner told me that's the one for $135 had pedigree papers, but the one for $85 did not. I opened up both cages holding one puppy in my left hand while the other in my right hand and put them back into the opposing cages.

I purchased the one for $85. That was Pierre. I thought I got a great deal only to discover after a few days that Pierre had a high fever and needed to be taken to the veterinarian. Ten days later, I came to pick him up and was handed an invoice for $110. Even with that, Pierre was a bargain once you got to know this incredibly sweet and smart puppy.

Once a week I would write a note and pin it to Pierre's collar and send him to Marlene's house just three blocks away. He had to cross street after street and was smart enough to wait until the traffic light was GO. He would walk up to the door at 5114 N. 11th Street and hit it with his paw. If no one promptly answered the door, he would then bark summoning Esther, my future mother-in-law, who welcomed Pierre in and gave him a cookie. Marlene would give the dog hugs and kisses along with a reply note to me. He would make the round-trip and bark at the door to come in.

At home on 8th Street, was parked a 1954 Packard Panama two door hardtop in brilliant red with handsome interior of red leather trimmed seats and black pleated cloth inserts that had silver thread running throughout. I purchased the car from Superfine Motors on Broad Street for $300. It was a beauty, but at the time I did not notice there was rust coming from a section on the rear fender. I had advertised the car for $475 but could not sell it. The advertisement ran out and I had planned to advertise again when I returned from our honeymoon.

Everything seemed fantastic surrounded by all the opulence in and around the Fontainebleau Hotel. Marlene and I rented a 1960 Thunderbird in Colonial white with red and white leather interior and a sunroof to visit various places of interest.

One could not walk outside of the hotel without gasping for breath since early July was hitting record high temperatures. We drove to traditional sightseeing venues and visited the parrot jungle among other sites. There were lots of other places which I can no longer remember since I still had business turning through my mind and quite frankly didn't have any interest in seeing parrots, monkeys or alligators wrestling.

After a couple of days I felt like I was coming down with something but did not know what it was. A couple days after that, I started to get the chills and felt feverish to such an extent that on a Saturday night I drove to the closest hospital. As I entered Mount Sinai Hospital, one of the finest hospitals in the area, a doctor in scrubs was exiting. I went to check myself in and was told that there were no doctors available at that moment and that the last doctor had just left as I was entering. Even as a kid I could not believe there was a hospital that had no doctors in an emergency room, but this just happened to

Lemon Juice

be in between shifts, so it appeared as if the hospital was devoid of doctors.

I was sweating profusely, which had nothing to do with the exterior temperature in Miami. I then noticed what appeared to be a doctor at the other end of the hallway. It was no apparition, it was in fact a doctor! He came in that Saturday night with his nephew, who had a broken arm. The boy had an x-ray and the doctor personally put a cast on the boy's arm because as it turned out, that doctor was an orthopedic surgeon. I asked for his help. He ushered me into the room where he had just put a cast on his nephew's arm.

My temperature was now 102°. He gave me some pills and told me to go back to my hotel and stay in bed, drink plenty of fluids and assured me in the day or two I would feel fine. Two days went by with me shivering and unable to swallow. I couldn't even eat a little Jell-O. I had the concierge get me a doctor no matter the cost. An hour later a doctor arrived, gave me some type of injection. He also gave me pain medication to help me swallow. The medication worked to the extent that I could eat only a little Jell-O, but at least that was nourishment. I don't recall exactly when the doctor got back to me, but he called to tell me that I had mononucleosis coupled with a staphylococcus laryngitis.

Flying home was no breeze but the antibiotics were helping, albeit, only a little bit. Bobby contacted his doctor who was able to see me. He took some bloodwork. I still felt pretty weak, however it felt good getting back into my bed back in Logan. After we were married, Marlene and I bought new furniture, Now there was a king-size bed to replace the pair of twin beds my brother and I slept in for years. My brother, Mickey, had married and lived with his new bride, Nancy.

Laying in bed was by orders of the doctor who told me it could take up to six months to recover from mononucleosis, also known as "the kissing disease." It seemed that our marriage was off to a terrible start since the doctor believed that I caught Mono in the reception line kissing everyone there. That, coupled with staphylococcus laryngitis really did me in.

I had just enough strength to walk to the bathroom. I realized subsequently that the medication for pain in my throat was Darvon. I think it was a pink and gray capsule. That, at least got me to the point that I was able to eat scrambled eggs and oatmeal, even though it constantly felt as if there was a lump in my throat. I just had to eat slowly.

My mother came up to the bedroom and asked if I noticed the 1954 Packard was not in front of the house anymore, which I had not noticed, having been feeling so ill. She told me she had sold it. I was really relieved since I could not get a buyer, which was unusual for me. She said she had placed a call to the newspaper classified section and told them to insert the advertisement for the Packard once again but this time to raise the price to $585. She sold it for that price. Then she gave me a bit of business advice: "If you have something to sell and you're not able to find a customer, do not reduce the price, for if you do, any potential customer will feel there's something wrong with the car. If you raise the price, you will get more activity because people will call to say the price was lower before. Then they will argue with you that they saw the lower price before. My response to them was that "we found out the car was being sold too cheaply." I will never forget that excellent advice she gave me nearly 60 years ago, and I have followed her guidance throughout my commercial real estate activities as well.

As with the theatrical phrase: "The show must go on," downstairs was Bobby selling cars and I was upstairs recuperating in bed feeling useless. I think it was either a '56 or '57 DeSoto that he sold the first day that I was laying in bed.

A few weeks went by that seemed like years to me, when I finally got enough strength to get dressed on my own accord and walked downstairs. I opened the front door and walked outside breathing in the fresh air, feeling blessed by the sunshine. Less than one minute later I was exhausted and had to slowly make my way back up the two flights of stairs and fell into bed. I could not believe what I was going through. So much in life was passing me by while I lay there doing nothing and producing nothing. Gradually, I got better and I was back to work hustling my ass off to make up for the several weeks that I was unproductive.

My engagement ring to Marlene as you now know was not a traditional diamond encrusted ring, but a small black curly haired French poodle named Pierre. To say he was a genius would be an understatement. When I did the switch at the pet store and took him home from the pet shop, finding out later that he had fever, I nursed him back to health in my basement office in Logan. To keep him warm, I placed my niece's baby

Marlene and Matilda

clothes on him. I heated his food and fed him multiple times a day, literally using a baby spoon. During the night I would go from my bedroom on the second floor to the basement to check on him. We certainly were forming a lifetime bond.

After Pierre recovered from his high fever, I went to the veterinarian's office on old York Road to pick him up. Ten days at the veterinary hospital plus a wash and a trim cost $110.00. I was shocked at the exorbitant expense, but paid the vet bill without complaint. I was so happy to have Pierre well again. Then, the vet went into the back room and came out with some little dog that looked like a poodle, but certainly was **not my** dog. I told the vet that was not my dog, to please bring out **my** dog. He told me that **was** my dog. An argument ensued. "That is not my dog!" He insisted that it **was**. I told him **no** and that I had no idea whose dog it was, but it certainly was **not mine!**

He told me to call the dog by his name. I reluctantly called out "Pierre" and the little black puppy who I was disavowing, jumped for joy. It **was him** but dressed in a French poodle show-clip and not my little round ball of fur. Eventually I got used to his decorative body as we spent day and night together.

I don't know why without thinking how stupid I was as a kid, I thought of pinning a note on his collar and instructed him to go to Marlene's house, yet he understood perfectly. I never restricted his outside movements because I didn't think anything that he could do would be a concern to me. I would simply open the door and let him go out to do his 'business' never thinking that he could walk in the street and get killed, especially with the higher traffic on Lindley Avenue with the 'J' bus passing our house every 15 minutes, rattling the windows throughout.

So, once a week I would send a note to Marlene and she would reciprocate by sending one back with Pierre, who was becoming our slow moving pony express. Everyday he would join Marlene and I as we went looking for automobiles to purchase.

On the 6600 block of N. Broad Street was Harold B. Robinson's Dodge dealership and an auction that he ran for wholesalers on Tuesdays. There were two lanes of cars running at the time. One of the auctioneers was Jack Sherry, who besides being an auctioneer was the best interior shampoo artist that I have ever seen. He could take a car with a cloth headliner that was black and from cigarette smoke and make it look like brand-new. I'm sure no one called him an 'artist' back then, but he was and taught me how to do it as well.

I introduced Jack Sherry to Pierre and after a few times that both Pierre and I went to the auction - and I was going from one lane to another, I handed Jack my auction identification card and told him that Pierre is going to bid on the car for me. I told Pierre to sit down and not move more than 4 feet from where the cars pulled up to a stop as the auction would begin. Seriously, he did not move one inch. He understood everything to the point that I could have a conversation with him as I would with an adult, but he was more intelligent than most of the adults I knew.

Marlene and Matilda

"Sold to Pierre," Jack brought down the gavel and yelled to me in the other lane. "He bought the car!" The dealers witnessed what was happening but never realized that I told Jack I wanted to buy the car no matter what.

In 1962 or 1963 we rented a house for the summer in Margate, New Jersey on Pembroke Ave. It was halfway between the ocean and the bay. A lovely home. I had purchased a 23 foot Chris Craft Continental mahogany speedboat and rented a boat slip one block from the house we were renting. Our first child, Ellen was a baby at that time. Pierre was growing up too. Everyday I would take our speedboat "My Marlene" out for a cruise. The finish on it was spectacular as I had previously taken it down to the bare wood and refinished it to be like brand-new. As I think about the interior I believe it was 1963 since I copied the interior from a new Lincoln Continental and placed it inside my speedboat.

Marlene could not tolerate going out on the boat since the rocking motion was making her nauseous. She took our daughter, Ellen, to the beach along with our mother's helper. I took Pierre with me and started the Chrysler powered engine in my Chris Craft and steered out to the ocean through the breakwater and headed toward where Marlene would be on the beach in Margate.

After spotting Marlene on the beach I dropped anchor staying far enough away that I was beyond the breaking waves. I instructed Pierre to stay there while I swam to shore. I don't think I spent more than 15 or 20 minutes talking to Marlene and playing with my baby, then swam back to the

Lemon Juice

boat. Boy, one can do stupid things when they're young and I certainly stretched that into my early adulthood.

I was swimming against the tide and it seems like for every two strokes forward the current was pushing me one stroke back. I could not believe how difficult it was to swim back to the boat when it was so easy heading to shore. If it wasn't for Pierre looking over the stern of the boat for me, I don't think I could have mustered up enough energy to make it back. Every ounce of my energy was expended to get to him. When I finally got to the stern of my boat, I was exhausted. I could not find the energy to lift myself out of water to get into the boat. Then, Pierre came over to the starboard [*right*] side and looked over the gunwale [*the upper edge of the side of a boat*] into my eyes. I grabbed onto a cleat [*a T-shaped metal protrusion to which ropes are attached*], pulled myself out of the water and into the boat lying on the deck exhausted. I apologized to Pierre and he accepted graciously. About a half-hour later I pulled the boat into the slip and tied up. We both got out and went to our rented home to rest.

In 1967 Marlene and I took a vacation to Acapulco, Mexico leaving Pierre with my mother in Logan. There was absolutely no concern about him. After spending about a week or so we took a flight back home. The first thing that I did upon landing was to grab the phone to call my mother. "Mom. How is Pierre?" She was livid that I did not ask her how **she** was and I did not know why. She told me that Pierre was not at her house in Logan but was with Mickey, my brother, in Northeast Philly, which was about one mile from our new home in Huntingdon Valley.

I pulled up to Mickey's house on Laramie Lane and knocked on the door at about 7 o'clock that evening. Mickey opened the door and from the doorway I could see down the hallway to where there was a recreation room on the right and a kitchen to the left. Laying on the floor at the farthest point from where I was, laid Pierre. "Pierre! Come here boy," I called to him, but Pierre did not respond. He laid there motionless. I could easily see he was visibly upset with us because we had left him. I walked over to him laying on the floor and cuddled him. I assured Pierre that I loved him. I could not believe that he wasn't excited to see me, but actually seemed upset that I was there. "Mickey. What happened to Pierre?" Mickey told me what had transpired:

When we left for our vacation we left Pierre in my mother's care. He spent his first year at our home in Logan and then the following years of his life at our new home in Huntington Valley, where each weekend my mother would spend with us. She loved him and he loved her. After the first day at his old home with my mother, my mom let Pierre out to do his business, which was no problem except that day. He disappeared. My mother was panicking. Where could he be? She did not know what to do or where to search for him. My mother was afraid that something happened to him.

Less than a mile from her home was Estate Liquidators, adjacent to Old York Road. We had our indoor showroom there and less than 150 feet from our office was where my aunt Ida lived. I had a large office there that I shared with my partners, plus in that same office were four salesman's offices.

My brother Mickey was running the business while I was on vacation with Marlene. He was talking to some customers and walked into the office only to see Pierre there laying on the floor in front of my desk! Mickey thought nothing of it believing that my mother had stopped by and left him there while she went to see her sister-in-law. That never happened. One hour went by and Mickey started getting concerned about my mother's whereabouts and called her home. She answered and told Mickey about Pierre's disappearance. Mickey bought Pierre back to our mother's house. She was so relieved seeing Pierre, that she started crying.

She watched him diligently when he went out to do his business on the small strip of grass that bordered her home. After a couple days when she felt comfortable leaving him to his own devices, he disappeared. No, he did not go back to Estate Liquidators. He was gone. The first thing my mother thought about doing was placing an ad in the Philadelphia Inquirer describing the dog, stating that he needs his medication and offering a $5.00 reward. Later, I asked why she put only a $5.00 reward in the paper. She told me that if it was a larger amount, somebody would think they had something valuable and would not return the dog. However, if it was very small amount they might have thought the dog needed medication and they would respond to her.

She was absolutely right. As soon as the newspaper hit the streets, she received a call from someone that lived near

Marlene and Matilda

Cheltenham Avenue. They did in fact have Pierre. He was taking the exact route that we took weekly when we picked up my mother to spend the weekend with us. My mother could not take the stress any longer of caring for Pierre, so Mickey agreed to bring Pierre to his house until we could pick him up.

That night with suitcases in hand, Marlene, Pierre and I were back home in Huntington Valley. Pierre was still not talking to me. I brought him up to my bedroom and patted him all night long. I could not sleep knowing that my dog was upset with me, until I finally dozed off at 6 o'clock in the morning. I was awakened by a sock across my face by his paw. "Pierre, you're back!" I was so excited that he was his old self again - and so was I.

I don't remember ever having a leash for Pierre. He was always let loose and always listened to everything we said. One winter in Huntington Valley he was out doing doing his business in the neighborhood, but this particular day he must have gotten the scent of a German shepherd in heat only one block away. There was no chance he could mate with the female shepherd because she was enclosed inside a cyclone fence. Pierre spent hours pacing around the cyclone fence looking to get laid. No such luck for him that night.

It was getting late and he hadn't come back home. It had been snowing for a day and finally let up. Snowplows came down our roads leaving huge mounds of snow alongside the sidewalks. Since everyone had driveways and a minimum of two car garages, no one ever needed to place their car on the street. That made it easier for the snowplows.

Lemon Juice

I opened the rear window of my bedroom and start shouting for Pierre to come home. It was close to 10 o'clock at night and a black dot was drawing closer and closer in my field of vision from the rear window. I had no doubt it was him. He came walking slowly until he reached the corner where our house was located. He was now attempting to get into our property but was faced with this 4 foot high mountain of snow that was probably a minimum of 5 feet wide at the base and formed a triangle of sorts. He stood there as I was now peering out of the front windows of the house. I gave him instructions: "Pierre, dig a tunnel." I repeated it one more time which was all that was necessary. Digging through from the street side a half a minute later or possibly more, out peered his black nose covered with snow. He walked slowly as he approached the front door entrance where we greeted him. He had large balls of snow and ice around each paw. We wrapped him up in sheets and towels and lifted him up and put him in the tub where we defrosted him, carefully making certain that we did not do it too quickly.

He never experienced any kind of sickness nor illness, other than when he was a puppy from the pet store. However, when he reached 13 years of age, he went out to do his business and never returned. To this day we cherish his memory and still wonder whatever happened to our Pierre.

Beside my wife, Marlene, the other important person in my life, you might have guessed, was my dear mother, Matilda (Billie).

Approximately 18 months after selling cars from my house I needed some help. There wasn't enough time in the day for me

Marlene and Matilda

to make all my stops, locate automobiles, make arrangements to have them delivered or picked up, plus having them detailed. I placed an ad in the Philadelphia newspaper for an auto porter. The job would pay $50 a week. I had quite a few applicants, settling on Bernie Moore. He was a young black man in his mid 20s with a nice personality and a willingness to work, with a good attitude.

I really didn't have enough work to keep someone busy 40 hours a week, but since Bernie was so pleasant and I enjoyed being around him - and considering I was making a darn good living, I could not let him go or cut his hours.

Everyday when I got a fresh car in, Bernie would clean the engine compartments, compound and wax the automobiles. Even with that, there was plenty of time left over each day, so I figured out something to keep him busy. My mother, Matilda (Billie) Helen Epstein, was employed at a lumber and millwork company on Old York Road in North Philadelphia. Her salary was the same as Bernie's, $50 a week. My mother's job was operating the PBX telephone switchboard, plus secretary to the president, Jules. She liked her work and never complained, even though her nerves were shot and one eardrum was thought to be partially punctured.

She used to take the "J" bus that ran East and West to Old York Road, then she would take the trolley car South to her job. Because of my tight schedule, especially while attending high school, I was not able to drive her to work. However, whenever possible, I would pick her up from work and drive her home.

Lemon Juice

Now, as a prosperous kid I purchased in 1955 Cadillac limousine in very nice condition with the thought of reselling it, but in the meantime I could put it to good use. I purchased a chauffeur's hat and black jacket for Bernie. He would be my mother's chauffeur.

My mother simply could not accept that idea. She liked Bernie and felt uncomfortable being chauffeured to and from work. I insisted. I told my mother that if Bernie could not take her to work and bring her home I would have to fire him because I don't have enough work for him merely cleaning cars. She reluctantly gave in.

Every morning Bernie would be at my house waiting for my mother to come downstairs and out to the car. She hopped in the rear seat with her lunch in a brown paper bag. In the evening, Bernie would drive her back home until one day my mom said that she could not go to work in the limousine anymore. She felt too uncomfortable about it. She also felt uncomfortable having Bernie chauffeuring her.

One day as they left to go to work, I saw my mother open the rear door where she was seated and hop out, getting into the front passenger seat next to Bernie, cuddling her bagged lunch. It was her way of telling him that they were equals.

I was totally upset that my mother still had to work and asked her on numerous occasions to please quit work. However, each time she refused. Then she refused to go in the limousine at all. She was okay with me picking her up in one of my cars, so I agreed to do that.

Marlene and Matilda

Her PBX office was situated facing the entrance, which had a pair of double doors. I had purchased a BMW Isetta, which at best is a mini-car. The entrance to the car was through a front door that swung open outwardly. It was a three wheel vehicle with two wheels in the front and one in the rear. I opened the double-doors to her office while my mother was sitting at the PBX board looking at me and then I drove the BMW onto the curb and into her office with the front of the car just a couple feet away from where she was seated. She was furious with me. "You're going to get me fired!" she said forcefully without yelling. "Yes, that's my intention…" I responded.

Driving home that evening, she was glad that she did not have to take public transportation, but was still upset with what I had done. "Please don't pick me up in a car like this again," and I agreed. The following day I had purchased another smoking Studebaker. I added some oil to the gasoline to exacerbate the smoke and it worked like a charm. I went to pickup my mother. I got into the Studebaker and raced the engine. Immediately there was no visibility behind the automobile. "What are you doing? Get me out of here!" she command - and so I pulled the car over to the side of the road, still staying on Old York Road to the next trolley stop. I then let her get out and waited for the trolley. Once she boarded the trolley, I positioned my car in front of the trolley and drove very, very, very, very slowly while periodically racing the engine. Later, my mother apprised me of just how upset the trolley car driver was and again, she was furious with me. But, she still refused to quit work so I had to take even more drastic actions.

Lemon Juice

A couple days later I placed a telephone call to Jules, her boss. I told him that she has ear damage and her nerves are shot from working there. I asked him to please fire my mother. "She's the best employee we have ever had here. I couldn't do without her," he stated. Once again I asked him to fire her. He refused. I said "Look, Jules, if you don't fire her, I'm going to kill you, plain and simple - you make the decision. If you don't fire her tomorrow, make sure you provide good plans for your family."

The following day my mother came home from work extremely upset because she was indeed fired. I told her "You're never going to work another day in your life. You're never going to have to worry about finances again either - not ever. You're my Mom. I'm going to take care of you." And so I did.

No one could ever ask for a better mother than my two brothers and I had in Matilda Helen Epstein aka 'Billie,' which she loved to be called. That was a nickname she acquired in her teens, since people compared to her to a famous actress at the time named Billy Burke.

My mother had her own flair for writing poems that expressed her feelings about her love for her family as well as world events. She was an avid reader and a person who cared more for others than she did for herself. No matter what I did wrong, and I did plenty, she was there to stick up for me and protect me, for I was her angel. She would never let anyone speak negatively about her children or anyone that she cared about. And she cared about plenty of people. Looking back today

Marlene and Matilda

at all the events that she went through before and after my father's death, I have no idea how she held things together - and yet she never once complained.

My mother was the matriarch of our family and her first thought was that she wanted her three children to aspire to greater things in life. She made certain that my brother, Milton Beryl Epstein, would continue with his music career, since he was one of the finest pianists in the country before he was drafted during the Korean Conflict. Because of his musical talents, he formed a band and was assigned to Nice in southern France, where he and his band entertained the troops.

I owe a wonderful life to my mother. Together, we worked through what others would have felt were insurmountable problems. Yet, together, we created a synergy that molded us into an exceedingly strong team.

In my mind's eye, I can see my wife, Marlene, pushing a baby carriage with her niece Bonnie in it, from her house on 11th Street to our home on 8th Street, just three short blocks away. Marlene was wearing pinstriped overalls that made her look like a sexy train engineer. As I had previously mentioned, but it's worth mentioning again, my mother fell in love with Marlene the first time they met - and from then on, they spoke with each other daily. Marlene felt the same way toward my mother. They were inseparable from that first day on, until the day of my mother's passing at the age of one hundred and four years.

I literally owe my life to my mother for her will was so strong that she would not let her new baby die even though she

Lemon Juice

was risking her own life. When we were losing our home, she would not give up and found an apartment in Northeast Philadelphia with a vacant beauty shop to rent, which she wanted to transform into a candy store with patent medicines. She rented out our house so that it would cover the mortgage payments, while we were living in an apartment above what was "Tabor Sweetshop." After one year of operating the candy store, she sold the business and made a $2,500 profit, which was enough to reclaim our home in Logan.

While in business at Broad Street Auto Center, I was purchasing automobile supplies for our inventory and a distributor named Bob had approached me with a proposal. He had two round trip tickets to Europe and Israel for 15 days to sell at a heavily discounted price. I could not afford the time away to take a vacation from our business so I called my mother and asked if she would like to go on this trip. She was thrilled, however, since my father had died she refused to date anyone. Her sister-in-law, Ida, who lived one mile from our house was a 'Spinster.' She was retired from the United States Army WAC and was commander at the local Veterans center. I knew my mother would feel uncomfortable about going on this lengthy trip alone, and I knew she had a good relationship with my aunt Ida. But Ida didn't have much in the way of savings that she could expend on this expensive trip. Instead of asking Ida if she wanted to go along on this trip and pay her share, I told Aunt Ida this trip was a gift from my mother. She was excited to have this once-in-a-lifetime opportunity to tour Europe and Israel.

Marlene and Matilda

In late 1960, I purchased the first 1961 Lincoln Continental convertible that was to come into the Philadelphia zone. It was an absolutely gorgeous automobile and the revival of the four-door convertibles from years past. My mother and Aunt Ida's luggage were packed into the trunk with very little room to spare. Both of my brothers accompanied us as we drove from Philadelphia to Newark Airport.

For many years my mother spoke about the wonderful time she and Ida had in Europe and especially in Israel. Countless times they described the places they had visited and the people they met, including the taxi driver in Tel Aviv, named Nachem.

Years later, both Marlene and I, through our charitable foundation, built and donated the Beit Guvrin Reservoir in Basor, Northern Negev, Israel, dedicated in my mother's name.

Never a day passes that we don't think about my Mom.

Lemon Juice

Gene's Maternal Great-Grandparents Marsha
and Jacob Lewis Axelrod c. 1900

Marlene and Matilda

Gene's maternal grandfather Max Lipschutz'
WWI Draft Card 12 Sept 1918, page 1

Lemon Juice

REGISTRAR'S REPORT

37-7-5. C

DESCRIPTION OF REGISTRANT

HEIGHT			BUILD			COLOR OF EYES	COLOR OF HAIR
Tall	Medium	Short	Slender	Medium	Stout		
21	22 ✓	23	24	25 ✓	26	Blue	Brown

28 Has person lost arm, leg, hand, eye, or is he obviously physically disqualified? (Specify.)

Rupture, Heart Trouble.

31 I certify that my answers are true; that the person registered has read or has had read to him his own answers; that I have witnessed his signature or mark, and that all of his answers of which I have knowledge are true, except as follows:

[signature]

Date of Registration Sept 12 1918

Local Board for
Division No. 13,
1429-35 N. 8th St.,
Philadelphia, Pa.

(STAMP OF LOCAL BOARD)

(The stamp of the Local Board having jurisdiction of the area in which the registrant has his permanent home shall be placed in this box.)

Gene's maternal grandfather Max Lipschutz'
WWI Draft Card 12 Sept 1918, page 2

Marlene and Matilda

Gene's mother Matilda "Billie" Epstein, 1943

Lemon Juice

Gene's family, back row from l-r: his father
Sam, older brother Wesley
Front row l-r: Gene, his mother Matilda and
middle brother Milton, 1945

Marlene and Matilda

Gene's father, Sam, at his used car lot,
"Wild West Auto Ranch" c. 1947

Lemon Juice

Where it all started c. 1955

Marlene and Matilda

Gene and Marlene, 1959

Lemon Juice

Gene and Marlene on their wedding day,
3 July 1960
Northwoods Catering, NE Philadelphia, PA

Marlene and Matilda

Gene Epstein in his "office" at the
Broad Street Auto Center, November 1961

Lemon Juice

Bobby Gordon at Northeast Autorama
early 1960s

Marlene and Matilda

Cadillacs

CADILLAC '58 LIMOUSINE Complete with all facty equipmt. Incl. Factory air-conditioning. 16,000 orig. ml. Factory list price $12,882.

SALE PRICE $1299
NORTHEAST AUTORAMA

Roosevelt blvd. & Levick st. PI 4-5030

CADILLAC '60 Fleetwood, complete with all Cadillac extras, including Durham top. Factory list price $7385. Magnificent car in every respect.

SALE PRICE $2299
NORTHEAST AUTORAMA

Roosevelt blvd. & Levick st. PI 4-5030

CADILLAC '61 Convertible. Full power. Truly magnificent in every respect. 18,000 orig miles. Like new.

$50 DOWN—$72 MO.

NORTHEAST AUTORAMA
Roosevelt blvd & Levick st PI 4-5030

Courtesy of The Philadelphia Inquirer

Lemon Juice

CONTINENTAL '63 sdn. A most magnificent auto in new cond. All power options including factory air. Gorgeous burgundy exterior with contrasting black & white leather trim interior.
$100 DOWN $73 A MONTH
NORTHEAST AUTORAMA
Roosevelt Blvd at Levick   Pi 4-5030

CONTINENTAL '57 Mark II. Air-cond. All power options, mint cond. No offer rejected. Call Pi 4-5030 for details
NORTHEAST AUTORAMA
Roosevelt Blvd at Levick   Pi 4-5030

Courtesy of The Philadelphia Inquirer

'64 PONTIAC
9 PASSENGER
Magnificent lime finish with white top & matching leather interior. Complete with all factory powers. Driven very few miles by past owner. Can be financed for
$10 DOWN $42 MO.
AUTO DISCOUNT CENTER
ESTATE LIQUIDATORS
Call Collect Phila. DA 9-7700

Courtesy of The Philadelphia Inquirer

Marlene and Matilda

Sign at Northeast Autorama
Courtesy of Gene Epstein

Lemon Juice

Northeast Autorama
Courtesy of Gene Epstein

Marlene and Matilda

Marlene and Gene aboard the
Formal Affair, 1986

Lemon Juice

Matilda Epstein aboard the Formal Affair, 1990.
She was 84 at the time.

Marlene and Matilda

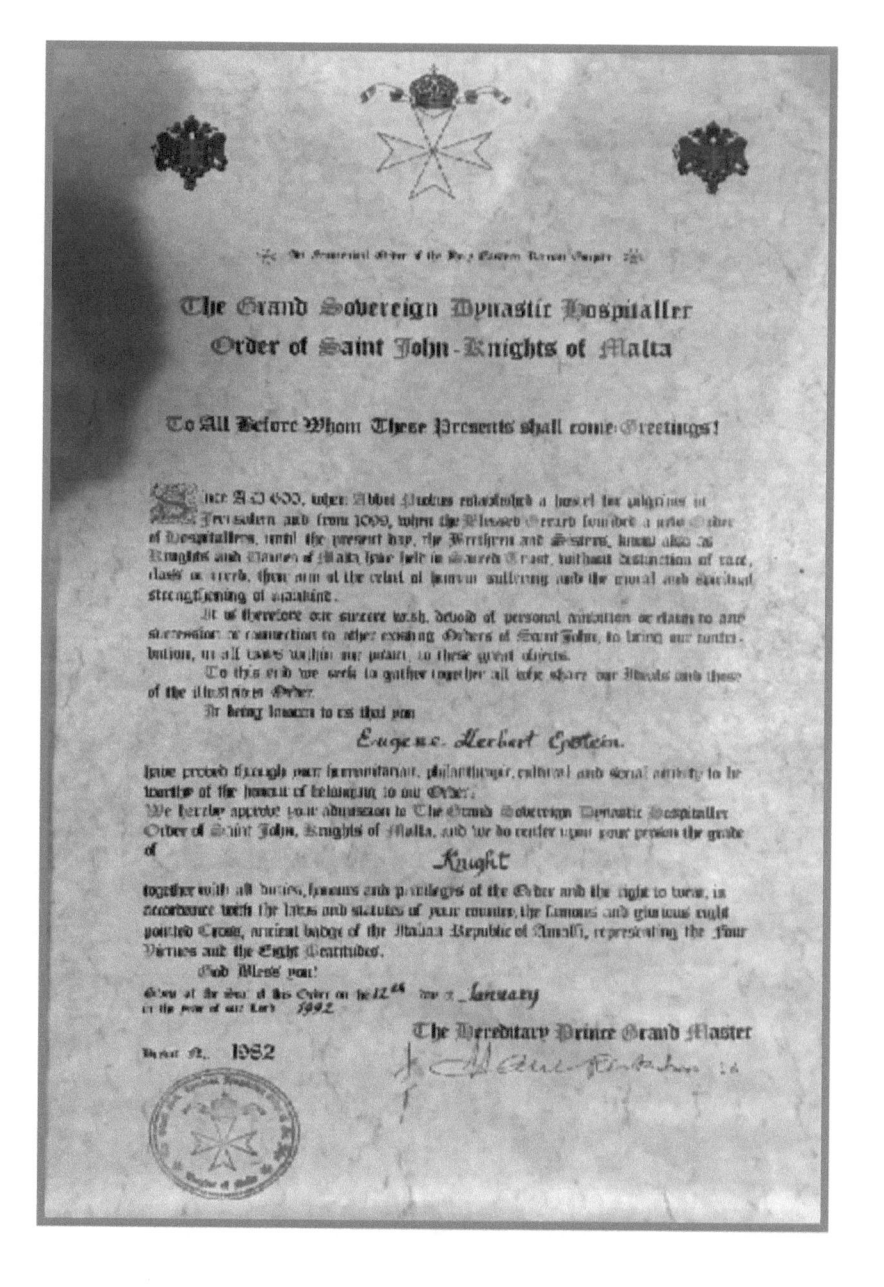

Proclamation from the Order of Saint John, Knights of Malta, knighting Gene for his humanitarian and philanthropic works,
12 January 1992

Lemon Juice

Dame Marlene being congratulated by
Prince Henri upon being knighted,
12 January 1992

Marlene and Matilda

Gene's brothers Wes (l) and Mickey (r).
Gene is standing in the center, 1992

Chapter Eight

My First Used Car Lot

At a service station which catered to car dealers in North Philly, I met a man who was interested in renting his car lot. This had a certain appeal to myself and my partner because the district attorney wanted me to stop selling cars from my home as a private party. The owner of the lease wanted to take a $150 loss on the monthly rental, and for me to pay the remaining $125 until the lease ran out. He could not make a living there as the last four owners went broke. I agreed to the terms because it was so inexpensive. Damn, it was cheap!

Broad Street Auto Center was Bobby and my first auto sales facility, established about 1961, commonly known as a used car lot. Neither Bobby nor myself had any knowledge about automobile financing. Established dealers have their connections and constantly advertised slogans such as "no money down," "easy credit," "only five dollars down," and the like. At "Broad Street Auto Center," we had mostly all cash sales. Our edge over those who were considered our competitors was that we were selling cars that appeared to

My First Used Car Lot

be at a very cheap price. In reality we were selling a less than first class car that was certainly worth less to purchase. Never did I realize during our first few months of operations that automobile financing was such an integral part of being successful in the automobile sales business.

Because of the proximity to our homes, Bobby and I did business with First Pennsylvania Bank and Trust Co., on North Broad Street in the Logan section of Philadelphia. It was equidistant between our homes and our car lot. A bank deposit could be made either going to work or on the way home. We had, prior to opening Broad Street auto center, done business personally with First Pennsylvania Bank. For a couple of years, I had auto loans with the bank and got to know the managers pretty well. Kevin was running the Broad Street branch and oversaw all the operations of the personal loan department. He was a straight-laced fellow, always peering down over his glasses.

At that time, First Pennsylvania was on a movement to go into direct competition with local finance companies and wherever possible opened up quick loan centers adjacent to those branches. If it were not available, they made room in existing bank facilities.

Seeing this new trend, Bobby and I spoke with Kevin about the possibility of doing business with them. He was very receptive, for this meant that any business that we were able to generate would be in addition to their targets. We made arrangements to get all the necessary forms from the bank such as credit application, finance contracts and bank notes. We had told

Lemon Juice

them that we sell a superior used car and since we sold them with a 12,000 mile guarantee, we were able to attract a first class clientele which avoided going to small loan companies. Kevin liked the idea and the next week we were phoning in credit applications.

Banks in general subscribe to a bank credit exchange. During the 1960s they were not permitted to do business with the retail credit exchange, which serviced finance companies only. This was to be our great advantage.

Before the first day was over, Kevin approved our first credit application. We had the customer sign the papers which were provided to us by the bank and the following morning I brought the signed papers along with my bank deposit. They were reviewed quickly by the loan officer and then deposited into our account. The nice thing was that in doing it this way, we did not have to bring the customer to the branch office as finance companies insisted upon, thus saving us hours of valuable time. It also meant that once the papers were signed, we had a deal. It really was like 'money in the bank.'

After a couple weeks our sales had increased because of this new source of financing, since, some of our customers did not have cash. It would also be another week or two when we were able to finance cars with HFC, which stands for Household Finance Credit, then, Greater Finance Company. The problem with the finance companies was simply that they would not approve as many deals as the bank did. They exchanged the credit applications and in most cases discovered that our 'superior' customer had in fact inferior credit. It was getting aggravating, taking so many of our applications but approving so few.

We started to advertise in the display section of the Philadelphia newspapers as did the other car dealers. We did that in addition to our classified advertisements, which specifically described our "sale" vehicles. Everyday we were taking more credit applications. One week there were very few approved loans. An officer from Household Finance stopped into our lot. He told us that our conversion rate was too high for it to be profitable doing business with us. The conversion rate was the amount of credit applications from them, compared to the amount which were approved. We had the worst of all dealers. Of the 23 applications that were submitted in one week, they did not approve even one. We were forced to do business primarily with First Pennsylvania. I decided what I could do to stimulate our business even more, was to place an advertisement with 'instant credit approvals' by your authorized First Pennsylvania Bank dealer. It appears as if the bank had authorized us to be a retail outlet. Credit applications were coming in all day long. We wanted the customers to come in person because it was a pain in the ass to have an approved deal without the customer ever coming in.

That week we received many applications from customers wanting to buy our cars and we sold plenty. It was primarily the same caliber customer however, because the bank was unable to exchange or check our past references with the exception of inquiring to see if the applicant lived and worked at the address, which was on the application, they gave us

Lemon Juice

most all approvals using "Redbook" as a guide. For example, if a customer was in his job more than two years and the retail value of the book was higher than the amount which we were requesting, they generally approved the credit. They didn't realize at the time that these customers by and large had poor financial credit. They seldom had bank credit because in those days someone with average or below average income ever thought of requesting a loan. Banks were for the rich - not for the average person. Since we purchased less than the average car in good condition, we paid less than the book price. This enabled our customer to buy a car from us with very little cash as a down payment.

When making purchases in those days it was a rule of thumb to place one-third down and finance the balance. If we were selling your car for instance, a 1957 Pontiac Safari worth $1,500 we could probably get $1,250-$1,500 financed for you. It also made some profit for us. The customer was happy because we were the only dealer that could secure financing for them. The bank was happy for all of the extra business without any effort on their part that they were receiving. It was a win-wn and great while it lasted. After the bank manager lost his promotion, they were checking into our car sales, wanting to see customers in person from then on.

Despite this little kink, our business prospered at Broad Street Auto Center, whereby it necessitated hiring an all around handyman, hence, Mr. Thompson stepped into our lives.

Abraham Charles Thompson was about 5 foot nine and a little bit on the chubby side. He was "colored" which was the

My First Used Car Lot

proper terminology back in the 1950s and 60s, always had a pipe hanging from his mouth. People who did not know him thought he had a surly attitude, while those that knew him better were absolutely positive he was surly.

Charles, as he was known, had one speed: Slow. He was however very punctual. Charles was the foreman, the detail person; the porter and the car washer of the infamous Broad Street Auto Center.

He was given his own private office because the "office" that we occupied was barely large enough to fit our overweight bodies. His office was a wood framed shack no larger than 5'x6' and had one poorly wired 50W electric bulb. We had tried to use a 100W bulb, however the wires started to overheat.

In the shack, was a kerosene heater vintage 1930. For ventilation, Charles would have to keep the door open. On the walls in his office were rows of shelving holding containers of aerosol paint cans which we used to brighten up the engine compartments. Also stored there were two 5 gallon cans of kerosene. Charles had a stool on which to sit. This completed his 'office.'

Charles was a prodder. He and I always got along well because I knew that I could not hire anyone to work day and night for less than $50 per week. There was however one benefit. He knew he had job security because we couldn't get someone to work for less.

Lemon Juice

Being that we did not have any covered areas in which to process our cars, all cars were scrubbed, polished and had engines degreased outside. In inclement weather, Charles had to make do. It didn't seem that there were too many rainy days, yet a couple stuck in my mind.

One day, Charles was looking lethargic as the clouds gathered and the rain came through. He knew that he would have to look like he was busy or else he would be summoned to do a high-speed polishing job with the electric buffer. There he was, looking toward our office feeling that my eyes were upon him. He pretended to be occupied but he was not fooling me.

"Charles, I have a customer coming up for the '56 Dodge Coupe," I yelled out from my office door. "Get it polished now!" I commanded. "Sheet…" he mumbled beneath his breath so that I could barely hear him.

There he stood with the electric buffer in his hand. The hood was the first to be polished when I noticed him going through the same motions he did every time he polished a car in the rain. "Ouch, mother, ouch," etc. The reason he did this was because the rain was coming down while he was using an electric buffer and was constantly being shocked.

This wasn't the first time this had happened, but it was the first time he got a real wallop and burned off all the hair on his arms. We let him take off the rest of the day and only docked him for a few hours.

My First Used Car Lot

Later that year, my cousin, Ricky, came to our car lot for a job. He was a young kid and the first day he came, it stormed. There was not enough room in Charles's 'office' so they both sat in a 1957 Plymouth sedan for refuge. The storm opened up and hail the size of tennis balls pounded the Earth. Then came the lightning. Looking skyward was like viewing an incredible fireworks exhibition. Lightning strikes followed lightning strikes with even more lightning strikes. Then one lightning bolt hit the car which was being occupied by both Charles and Ricky. I was scared and afraid to look inside. I was wondering what to say to my aunt Gertrude, Ricky's mother, fearing they were both fried to a crisp inside that Plymouth. Luckily, the rubber tires prevented them from sustaining life threatening injuries.

Charles had told me he needed a new garden sprayer canister which he used to spray motor degreaser in the engine compartment. We reluctantly purchased a new one. He put the parts together and filled up the unit, however he never tightened the hose clamp. I stood there watching the inauguration of our new piece of 'shop equipment.' He pumped it in order to build up sufficient pressure - and then it happened. The hose, which had not been secured tightly, flew off and the degreaser, which was under pressure escaped shooting directly into my eyes and mouth. I was instantly blinded and started screaming in pain. Bobby also got frightened. He guided me to my Lincoln convertible and drove me to the Jewish Hospital one mile away. There, I was rushed into the emergency room and treatment was instantly administered. They flushed my eyes but to no avail. I could not see. I was in pain and I was gasping

Lemon Juice

for breath from the degreaser residue which went into my mouth and lungs.

In an instant we were met by my two brothers and all four of us were on our way to Wills Eye Hospital, known globally as the finest eye care facility.

Bobby drove down Broad Street as fast as he possibly could. If there were any traffic he drove onto the center cement divide to pass the other cars.

I threw up on the floor and was in shock. Later, at Wills Eye Hospital, I was examined by two doctors who told me it would be be impossible to determine if I would ever regain my eyesight.

The pain had subsided somewhat and the realization had set in. I might be permanently blind. I was given eyedrops to freeze my eyes if the pain was unbearable.

Arriving at home, my two brothers stood one on each side of me. I had put on a pair of sunglasses to hide my eyes from my wife. I would try to make it through the night without her detection. I told her that my allergies were terrible and that my doctor gave me medication which made me sleepy. I went to bed and was very frightened. How could I make a living for my family? Who would take care of them? Who would help my children grow up? Who would pay the mortgage? I was sick with worry and fright.

My First Used Car Lot

The following morning my brothers took me to an eye specialist. The doctor and his father were world renowned ophthalmologists. He told me after scraping my eyeballs, he thought it was a miracle that the degreaser had burnt only the external tissue but not anything else. I trembled as he carefully scraped the burnt tissue away. He admonished me to sit still and not move my head no matter what or else or I would be permanently blinded.

My head remained still as I quivered inside. Three days later I was working Charles' ass as hard as he ever worked. We were both happy. I actually loved that guy and I think the feeling was mutual.

One day, I received a call from Chartreuse, Charles's wife. "Gene, Charles got into an accident on his way home last night." I was waiting for some bullshit story but it was unlike Charles to miss even one day of work. "He was driving his Ford and ran into the back of a city trash truck. He crashed through the windshield and slid over the hood into the back of the trash truck."

This was just too much to believe. "Gene," she continued, "Charles will be in to work tomorrow. He's in the hospital and getting his head stitched. He got 19 stitches but he will be in tomorrow." Now, who in the world could have been in an accident and thrust through the windshield of an automobile, smash his head, be thrown into the rear crusher of a trash truck and still be into work the next morning with 19 stitches? I could not wait for this charade to play out.

Lemon Juice

The following morning Charles appeared on time. He had taken the Broad Street bus since he was unable to drive his own Ford that had been aerodynamically reconfigured by 5 less feet. His entire head was wrapped in bandages. I insisted that he partially open up the bandages to show me his supposed 'wounds' - he did. This was not the Abraham Charles Thompson I knew. This was Mel Brook's version of Frankenstein.

From one section of this forehead to the other were a series of stitches. He looked like he had been mauled by a chainsaw. He told me the doctor advised him to take two aspirins twice a day for pain, but he didn't need them. If this had happened to me, I would have been in intensive care for over a month while being administered my choice of codeine or morphine. Charles detailed two cars that day and cleaned up my office.

For many years, even though he was no longer working for me, I would call to see how he and Chartreuse were doing. When I heard that he was having a tough go of it, I convinced my partner Bobby to have our company help him out financially. How could we not?

The size of our used car lot, Broad Street Auto Center, was about 75 feet in width by hundred and 25 feet in depth. The lot was originally part of a larger used car facility which was out of business and one-half of the property was sold to an automobile detailing and parts replacement franchise. The water line was on their side of the property, which meant that was extremely important to keep on good terms with my neighbor, as the good book states. This was not as easy

My First Used Car Lot

as it may appear. Both my brothers Mickey and Wesley had a similar business of their own in a different part of the city however it was close enough to service us. Besides, even if we were further away, I would have still given any business we had to them. Why not keep it in the family? This disturbed the franchise owner, Harry and in his own way, he let us know.

Subtle hints were dropped at the deli next door by him to reach us. It did very quickly. "I won't give them an ounce of water from my spigots unless they buy everything from me," he proclaimed.

The following day we presented him with a car that needed some work. I asked him to cut me a break because I have family in the business. He accommodated me with a lower price than he gave his other dealers. I still managed to give my brothers the bulk of the business and all went well for the time being - until little disturbances started to occur - and reoccur.

I noticed a freshly painted 1957 Ford four-door sedan with a light green exterior had been dented on the left side. A couple of other cars had little dents along the left side and some small body parts removed. It started to bother me because of the cost and inconvenience, therefore the investigator in me put on the traditional trench coat and deerstalker cap and started to snoop around. I spoke with a couple of Harry's workman who hated him because he was such a tyrant and sometimes quite a bit flaky. They told me he was aggravated that I was still giving my brothers work, especially because they were competitors of his; they both catered to the same trade.

Lemon Juice

The first damaged car was parked between both of our lots where there was a dividing line somewhere a couple inches on his side of the line. He did not need any extra room, for his lot was spacious enough for all the business he had and the area next to our cars was usually empty.

In looking at the damage again on the '57 Ford, I could see two round exhaust marks where the dents were situated. It could have been from any car with those exhaust marks, however these exhaust marks were definitely smaller than any traditional exhaust pipes. I almost didn't give it much thought, until one day I saw a 1952 Cadillac on his lot that had dual (twin) exhaust pipes, which came through the bumper. Cadillacs usually had an exhaust over 2 inches wide however this exhaust pipe was replaced with his stock item. Their stock exhaust pipes were much smaller. I measured the pipes on the Cadillac and then the circular exhaust marks on the 1957 Ford. It was a perfect match! Now on to Harry… "Hey Harry! Do you have any idea who ran their car into my Ford?" I asked in a gentlemanly way. "Why would you ask me?" He replied with an amused tone in his voice, as if to imply: 'Well, you didn't catch me!'

It was usual for him to park his cars perpendicular to mine and having them head-in with the front of his cars facing my lot. This car was not only backed in, but backed into my Ford.

I soon discovered that the car belonged to an employee of his. I then confronted his employee about it. He was a bit shaken but said that he had been using his other car for the past week and that Harry had been using his Cadillac. He knew

My First Used Car Lot

that Harry had done this damage to one of my cars, but Harry was still his boss and he was afraid to say more. He told me however that he would deny he spoke to me if ever confronted by Harry. I promise not to let anyone else know we spoke.

It wasn't worth reporting these incidents to the police, but it was certainly obvious that the entire row of our automobiles which sat on the border of the two properties were the only cars that were vandalized. Each damage was also too small to report to the insurance company, so I had to absorb the expense.

Harry's franchise opened up for business promptly at 8:30 every morning. By 10 o'clock his business was brisk and loaded with automobiles needing all sorts of detailing and parts replacement work. I am told that someone, possibly an upset customer or a disgruntled employee, placed telephone calls to stone quarries requesting 25 tons of stones that had to be delivered by 6:30 in the morning until one agreed. At 8 am arriving at my car lot, I drove past the franchise and was amazed to see in front of each garage a huge amount of crushed stone. Was he getting the place resurfaced? That would be surprising because it looked fine to me and I saw the parking lot everyday.

I enjoyed my cup of coffee and four scrambled eggs with melted cheese at Lou's Deli next door. I stayed there for my normal time and grabbed a Tastykake lemon pie and my favorite bag of Wise potato chips, paid my bill and left. As I walked past Harry's place, I saw one employee standing

Lemon Juice

on a mound of stone and the owner scratching his head in wonderment.

"What's going on Harry? Are you black topping your lot?" I couldn't resist letting him think that it might have been me who did this. My mother always spoke of me as being an angel but in her heart she certainly must have known differently.

I am told someone called the newspapers claiming they were Harry and placed an advertisement in the help-wanted section for some workers. It read as follows "Wanted - porters to clean offices and run errands. No experience necessary. No car. No references. Three dollars per hour starting. Apply Mr. Harry." The ad stated the address on N. Broad Street. To understand its true effect, one has to realize that times were rough and our economy was in a recession. The average wage at that time was only $1.25 per hour. The advertisement hit the newspaper just after their employees had finished cleaning up their lot, which had been filled with stones. And they didn't even blacktop it. What a waste of time and money!

The following day the advertisement had brought in a long line of people leading from their showroom door to what seemed like over the horizon. At least 100 people were waiting to get their personal interview with Harry. He was running up and down the line like a nutshell, screaming at everyone "Get out! Get out! I'm not hiring anyone. Everybody get out of here!!" It was not very nice of him yelling and ranting as he did. I walked up to a few people in line and told them that he was known to be crazy at times and just try to forgive him. I took that long

My First Used Car Lot

line of job applicants as an opportunity to sell those people a car, but made no sales.

"Christ Harry, you must be the biggest franchise owner in the country. One day you're stoning your lot and then you're hiring the world. I hope that my porter doesn't apply for a job at your place. I certainly could not afford to pay him that much." I turned and walked away. At one point I could feel his vibes shaking and I walked extra fast fearing that he would run over and take a swing at me, thinking that I was behind his troubles. If that were the case he should have taken his swing when he was able to, for the next week he was too busy. He must have really upset someone.

Everyday at least three insurance agents came to his office unannounced. From what was related to me, all received telephone calls from 'Harry' who informed them that he felt his life was over even though he was in the prime of health. He wanted a $1 million whole-life insurance policy. "Just come to my store whenever you can. You don't need an appointment. If I appear busy, please interrupt me. I want to take care of this matter immediately." How could any insurance agent worth his salt not go running out of the office grabbing hat and coat to meet with Harry? It was amusing seeing the salesman straighten their ties, fold their trench coat neatly over their arm, enter the showroom door. At first he spent up to 15 minutes talking with the insurance agents. The next day came and went with a new batch of insurance agents. Everyday another agent with a briefcase in hand approached the showroom

Lemon Juice

door until they were shoved out of the building. How erratic Harry's behavior was!

Not giving him time to relax, someone called the police department which was only a few streets away from Harry's store, crying hysterically into the phone: "Help!! He's dead!!! Just dead!!! Lying there with his tongue hanging out of his mouth!!!!! Oh my god!! He's really dead!!!!!"... "Relax Mister. Just take your time and relax," said the reassuring voice on the other end of the line.

The police officer asked for his name and address so that they could send over the city's morgue wagon. The person calling, as I was told, supposedly told him that the dead man was Harry_____, stating that he was just talking with him when he grabbed his throat, twisted and fell over. "Oh, I can't believe it. Quick officer. People are going crazy. The store is having a sale and everyone's walking around his body. Nobody wants him on the floor. Please get him out of here right away!!" The voice on the phone shrieked.

The police department was very close and within two minutes the patrol cars started pulling into their parking lot. A vehicle with lettering "City Morgue" pulled up at the same time and two officers jumped out with a stretcher wide open. We immediately went over to see what all the commotion was about.

"What the hell is going on? What do you guys want?" Harry directed his queries to all the cops as they were rushing into the showroom. "We're here to pick up the body of Harry

My First Used Car Lot

_____ stand aside." Needless to say, Harry's color. which previously had a healthy glow from being outdoors shoveling stone the past week, quickly drained from his face. He was getting paler by the minute. We quietly walked back to our lot and watched all the cars disperse. At the same time, I am told a wreath of flowers were ordered and delivered to his wife "In Loving Memory of Harry"…

All along I believe that Harry suspected we had done these things - or perhaps he knew who did it. Either way, we never had an argument or discussion after that. We had full use of the water and no other car was ever vandalized.

On the south side, next to our car lot was a piece of ground about 100 feet wide on Broad Street. It ran the full length of Broad Street until it reached Old York Road. The ground was elevated where the property line met our Used Car lot and a stone wall faced our property. I never paid attention to what was there until I crossed the street to where there was another Used Car lot. Broad Street was considered 'Used Car Dealer Road.' It was good for all the dealers to be known as the one area to do all your used car window shopping. There was a salesman who we never knew his real name, but he wore a top hat and wanted to be called "Colonel."

He had a particular, strange look about himself. He appeared at medium height with light brown hair and questionable build. His body looked as if he was wearing many, many shirts. And the reason for that was, because he was! Wearing all those shirts, he was one hot Kernel ready to pop. "Kernel Shirts," as we begun to refer to him, was the son of the previous owner

Lemon Juice

of the dealership. Part of the deal when his father sold the facility was that the new owners employ his son, who was quite eccentric.

As a kid, he must have fallen out of the crib and landed on his head. He really was wearing a minimum of five dress shirts at any one time. He denied it, but you could see sleeves and more sleeves sticking out from his wrists. One shirt color on the outside with plenty of different shirts underneath. It was obvious that he wasn't wrapped too tightly.

He told us about the piece of land between both our lots and he asked me if I had ever been through it. I reply that I never paid any attention and only thought it was an old lot. "Kernel Shirts," as he became known to us, was an authority on the American Revolutionary War. That vacant lot adjacent us that I never paid any attention to, turned out to be an historic American Revolutionary War cemetery. A very old graveyard that had the then Mayor of Philadelphia, Richardson Dilworth buried there. The graveyard was filled with American Revolutionary War soldiers' decayed bodies.

Some soldiers were from the Colonies while others were from England. Buried there was General Howell who died fighting in the Battle of Germantown. General Howell was buried in this cemetery as a courtesy ordered by General George Washington. All this was intriguing to me. I don't think people pay much attention to the small urban cemeteries with their historic backgrounds. Meantime, Kernel Shirts had shown us some brass buttons that he collected. He told us of their great value to collectors. It seems he may have been digging in

My First Used Car Lot

the cemetery, removing buttons from Revolutionary soldiers' military uniforms. I'm not sure he was telling the truth, but in my estimation, digging up graves that honored our Revolutionary War heroes was revolting and disrespectful. I tried to avoid Kernel Shirts whenever possible from that point on.

We offered for sale a 1953 MG roadster that was cream-colored with red leather interior. The car was spotless and functioned like new. We had $500 invested in the automobile and were asking $800 for it.

A doctor came by and wanted to buy the automobile for his son. He wanted to know our best price. I held firm onto the $800 price and he was the buyer since my price was less than what they were selling for at other dealerships. I don't think another car of that same model could be nicer.

The buyer informed me that he was a surgeon and operated at the Jewish Hospital, which was very close to our business. I told him that for quite a while I had something at the base of my spine that would ooze fluid. In our shack that we used as an office, he took a quick look at my lower back and said it was a "Pilonidal cyst," which he could remove.

After haggling back and forth a few times, we made a deal: He would perform the surgery, including the cost of the hospital expenses, if I sold the car to him for $500. The next week I was in the Jewish Hospital and he was operating. Times have changed greatly over the years as I would have been in and out of the hospital for same-day surgery today, however back then it was a nine day stay in the hospital.

Lemon Juice

Laying in the hospital shortly after the surgical procedure, I was concerned that I was not at my place of business. I called Bobby and asked him to bring over my Tower electric typewriter, which I purchased that year from the salesman in the typewriter department of Sears. I wanted a typewriter so that I could type up advertisements to place in the newspapers while Bobby was taking care of the business. Even though I could not stand or sit, I wanted to do something productive over the course of the nine days I spent in that hospital. I'm not one to sit idly by when I know I can conduct some business or do some ancillary work. When I returned to my place of business, I consummated the deal with the doctor who was excited to give this cute little MG roadster to his son as a gift. I was healed and everybody was happy!!

With all the advertisements that we were placing in the Philadelphia Inquirer and the Evening Bulletin our little used car lot on Broad Street was a place of constant activity. Between heading to the auctions two and even three times a week and running the business, plus still visiting the dealers that I had frequented previously to opening up our car lot, there wasn't much time to speak with customers, which was our bread-and-butter.

I met an automobile wholesaler, Dave, who was quite a pleasant person. He stood over 6 feet tall, with blonde hair, heavyset but not fat, who wore 'Coke bottle' eyeglasses. I asked Dave if he would be interested in selling cars on a commission basis at my car lot. Everybody knew how active we were and he was very interested. I had no idea if he could

My First Used Car Lot

sell an automobile and do the necessary paperwork that was part of every transaction. I offered him 10% on the net profits from any automobile that he sold. He agreed and I guaranteed him $300 even if he never sold a car in any given week.

I sat in my office looking out the window. There was Dave opening a door to a car showing it to a customer and then waving goodbye. "What was I seeing?" A customer leaving my car lot without buying a car? I quickly ran outside as the customer was leaving. I asked Dave what happened. He told me that wasn't a buyer, only a 'looker.'

As the customer was closing the door to his automobile to leave our property I stopped him and cajoled him back to the car he was looking at. Thirty minutes later, my porter was placing new temporary license tags on the car.

I told Dave anytime a customer comes into our lot, not only is the customer a buyer - but he's our customer and our buyer. "Never, ever let a customer leave this lot without bringing them to me if you cannot make a deal," I emphatically told Dave. Time after time he would just greet a customer and bring them to the office for me to make the deal. At the end of the first week I had to write a check out to Dave for $700 since we made $7,000 on the transactions. I handed him the check and fired him immediately. I didn't need anybody to say 'hello' and bring them to the boss to consummate the deal.

After we terminated Dave at our Broad Street location, we placed an advertisement for an **experienced** salesman. The job description emphasized "fully experienced with proven

Lemon Juice

references," however, one applicant who responded had no experience at all, but he was willing to do **anything** to get a job in the automobile business. Henry Burdumy, weighing in at 135 pounds and probably 5 foot 8" tall, was a wirey, hyperactive fellow who spoke 50 miles an hour.

After reading his resume, which contained absolutely nothing of interest, he was smart enough to add *"there is nothing I will not do to get this job."* I brought him in for an interview and hired him instantly. I then placed a telephone call to Seymour, the owner of a sign company, and ordered a sandwich-signboard that read: "**$5.00 DOWN at BROAD STREET AUTO CENTER**" in bold lettering printed on both sides of the Masonite panels. The 'sandwich boards' were painted with a black background and orange plus chartreuse Day-Glo paint for the letters. The two panels were attached with cloth straps so that Henry could walk up and back on Broad Street in front of our used car lot. But there was a hitch to Henry getting the job. If he really was willing to do *"ANYTHING"* for a job, I wanted him to walk naked wearing the signboards. I thought that would bring additional attention to our advertisement.

Henry had absolutely no hesitation, nor fear of embarrassment, as he stripped down to his bare naked body and slipped into the signboards with the straps sitting on his shoulders and his head protruding from in between the two boards at the center.

I don't think one hour passed before people were very close to colliding into each other as they drove by our Broad Street

My First Used Car Lot

Auto Center. Henry did not mind at all. In fact, I think he actually got a kick out of it — that is, until the police showed up.

"He can't be out there naked. It's against the law," the first officer exclaimed. I responded "Can you show me where the law states that a person cannot walk around with signboards covering their genitals?" It was 3:30 in the afternoon as the officer glanced at his watch. Instead of responding to me, he simply stated "You know what, let the next shift figure it out…" as he was intent on getting back to the police precinct to sign himself out of his shift by 4pm.

I thought Henry really had balls even though I never got to see them, but anyone who would subject himself to what I put him through, deserved the job. It turned out Henry became a fantastic salesman and we had plenty of fun together. Years later, he became extremely successful as an innovator in the auto junkyard reclamation business. Believe it or not, this is the stripped-down, stark naked version of this occurrence. Who would have thought this is what it took to get his career off the ground…

At the next auction my eyes were glistening as the red light above was blinking, signifying that the car on the block was being sold 'as is.' That meant one of a few things: There were several things that might be bothersome and the dealer did not want to have any arguments. Another could be that either the engine, the transmission or something major might need attention. One thing for sure is, the car had a good look about it and the engine sounded relatively quiet. Whoever the high

Lemon Juice

bidder was, he had no opportunity to road test the vehicle and had to pay for it immediately.

The car was a very good-looking 1957 Cadillac four-door sedan DeVille. The average wholesale price for a model like this in good condition was $1,200-$1,400. The price this car reached during the bidding was only $600... a steal. "Sold to Broad Street Auto Center," the auctioneer announced as he bought down the gavel.

When the car arrived at our car lot it performed pretty well driving from Bordentown, New Jersey to go to Broad Street Auto Center. We did hear a slight engine bearing noise, but one would have to be an expert to detect it. I was very satisfied with this acquisition and it was placed on the frontline for sale right away.

Within two days we received a $300 deposit on the car, which we were selling for $1,300 subject only to the customer's credit approval. In other words, if we could get his credit approved then we had a deal or the customer would forfeit his deposit. His application was submitted to First Pennsylvania Bank and within three hours we received a call that the applicant's credit was rejected due to 'poor past credit experience.'

"Dammit!" I thought. Missed that one! Within an hour the customer came strolling down the street heading toward our car lot. I greeted him at the front pavement. I was about to tell him that he was turned down for credit but I hesitated, wanting first to hear what he had to say. "Hey man! I decided not to buy the car because I just lost my job." I knew it was pure bullshit.

My First Used Car Lot

I immediately informed him that his credit was approved and should he not go through with the deal he would forfeit his $300 deposit.

When he heard that, he told me he was going to his lawyer, named Cecil Moore, to see about getting his deposit refunded. I told him that it wasn't worth my trouble, so if he wanted to forget the deal I would refund one-half of his deposit. However, if he insisted on going to an attorney, I would give him nothing.

We were both friendly and he realized what he originally agreed upon but still went to his attorney. The following day I received a call from someone whose voice sounded like it was coming through an echo chamber. It was the first time I had heard a voice through a squawk box. "My name is Cecil Moore and I want you to refund my client's deposit." I told him either get his client on the phone directly or stick it up his ass. An hour later my customer arrived asking for one-half of his money back - but I refused.

Looking back, it was really stupid of me to speak to Mr. Moore that way, but I didn't realize he was a famous attorney and well respected civil rights activist!

At that time in my life I wasn't thinking of anything except building up a business and making enough money to pay for that day's bills.

The customer returned, shook my hand and told me he should have accepted my first offer, because he really didn't lose his job. He purchased a car from my competitor three blocks

Lemon Juice

away. That was fine with me because I knew I would not have any trouble selling that really nice Cadillac.

The very next day, the 1957 Cadillac DeVille was sold to Robert Henderson, a small bandleader at a local pub.

When I say he was a 'small bandleader' I mean it, because he was diminutive in size, plus his band consisted of only three people and not one of them were over 5' 3" tall.

When Robert arrived that day, the moment he saw the Cadillac, his eyes lit up! He always dreamt of owning a Cadillac. Robert had no credit so we gave him some. We submitted his application to the bank and told them the price was $1,500 instead of $1,300 and that Robert was putting up $600 toward the down payment. We gave them references that they were unable to check. We also told the banker that Robert had been playing at the same local pub for nearly five years. The information looked good on paper and shortly thereafter his loan was approved.

The price that we were selling the car for was significantly less than the retail price but we would still make an excellent profit. The next step was to inform Robert of the information, which we gave to the bank, and prepare him when they would write the deal at the local office. We apprised him that we had raised the price $200 and it would appear that he was giving us more of a down payment than he actually was. In reality he was supposed to give us $300 and we were hoping for a bank approval of $1,200 however, they had only approved $1,000.

My First Used Car Lot

With Robert's $300 and the banks $1000 we still had our original $1,300 that we needed. We would be short only the money for sales tax and registration. We certainly did not mind because Robert could pay us out on a weekly basis as so many people had done before.

When Robert returned to our car lot after picking up the money from the bank, he handed me the check and said that he would pay us the $200 that we were short as soon as possible. He had believed that we were actually selling the car for $1,500. I told him I could not accept the extra $200 because that wasn't our deal. We stuck to the $1,300 we had agreed upon.

He proudly drove home in his newly acquired Cadillac DeViille with an enormous smile reaching ear to ear. On the way home Robert smashed the automobile into a telephone pole. No insurance whatsoever. Now what? We called the local body shop who estimated the damages to be about $600 including parts and labor. Now how the hell were we going to get our registration and tax money? A light in my head started to illuminate. When I called the bank, I told them that Mr. Henderson just stoped in and was talking to us about buying a piano which his neighbor had for sale. He could not get the cash because he just spent his money for car insurance. I told him that I recommended Robert to stop back at the bank to see if they would make him a $600 loan for the piano. For an automobile they would not give him another penny. For a piano, they would be glad to loan him the $600 in cash.

Robert made the trip to the bank once more and returned with $600 in cash. I immediately took the sales tax money

Lemon Juice

and registration out of the $600. "Robert, take some of this money and buy the parts to repair the car. Then go to the body shop and have them install those parts." He could not stop thanking me.

The following week Robert stopped by driving the Cadillac with the windshield smashed from the previous week's accident. "Hey Gene, take a look," he pointed to the rear seat where he had a fender and bumper jammed in. How happy Robert was that Sunday that he was able to put the car together without a single complaint. Some people were very easy to please. The 1957 Cadillac DeVille all together grossed a profit of $1,000 on a $600 investment.

Broad Street was always known as 'dealer's row' - a place where you could sell your car for quick cash. Every dealer had his sign outside which stated *"Top dollar for your car."* The average customer went from dealer to dealer trying to get the most money for his car. Some dealers offered a customer a ridiculous price for their car knowing full well that the customer was going to go shopping. If a customer returned for the dealer's super offer, the dealer simply pulled one of his excuses out-of-the-box to apply to the situation. "I really needed that car because I had a customer for it but since you left the customer purchased something else, however I can still pay a reasonable figure." What was reasonable to the dealer was not necessarily reasonable to the seller. Usually somewhere in between they struck a bargain.

One afternoon a customer came onto our lot to sell an MG roadster. We took the car for a test drive and made the

My First Used Car Lot

customer an offer. He told us that 'Big Moe' down the road offered him $200 more and he wanted $100 more than that. I told him that if Big Moe paid him what he had offered, then I would sell Big Moe my entire inventory and retire.

The seller of the MG drove to Big Moe's for the promised 'better deal.' He was once again greeted by Moe with the traditional pat on the back. I guess Moe felt that he was comforting the customer in advance of the operation that he was to perform on him. Moe told the seller that before he could pay the amount which he offered, he would have to test drive the customer's car.

Moe looked around and could not find his salesman nor his mechanic. They were both out at lunch. Moe was too fat to fit into the average size car let alone this small excuse for a car called an MG roadster. After the customer was tired of waiting, Big Moe tried to determine any problems with the car without attempting to drive it. He told the seller that it appeared to have a slipping clutch and a poor transmission, which the customer vehemently denied.

The seller was getting fidgety and told him that he wanted payment now or he was leaving. Moe needed to test drive the car because he really had someone interested in it and he could make a fast buck. Still looking around, Moe could not find his people who were able to determine if there was anything wrong with the car. So afraid to miss a deal, he opened the driver's side door and very slowly squeezed himself into the seat. In doing so he broke the back rest of the seat and was unable to close the driver's door. The steering

Lemon Juice

wheel was jammed into his stomach and Big Moe found that he was unable to move the pedals with his feet since he was squeezed in so tightly.

The customer started bitching that he better buy the car now because there was nothing wrong with it and besides, Moe had just broken the seat. Moe was sweating, not from the pressure of the seller, no, no, no customer ever got him sweating. He was sweating from the pressure of being wedged in the car and unable to move.

He started to breathe heavily. Moe thought that he was having a heart attack. The seller thought that they were both going for drive together so he had closed the driver's door and walked around to seat himself in the passenger seat. The closing of the door was the final nail in the coffin for Big Moe Wasserman. He was unable to move his hands, feet, arms and legs. He was packed in there tighter than a sardine in a can of King Oscar's finest.

The customer sat there, Big Moe sat there, when Moe started cursing. He would not do anything except curse. He told the seller to "stick this little fucking car up your ass," which got the seller very upset. The seller insisted that Big Moe get the hell out of his car and pay him to get the seat fixed. Big Moe tried to squirm but found that if he attempted to move even one part of his body, he was only forcing another part past its limits. Moe was stuck! He kept cursing the car and the seller.

Moments later, his salesman returned from lunch and Moe tore into his ass continuing his verbal assault - and out of

My First Used Car Lot

frustration told the salesman that he was fired." Fuck you fats! Get your own ass out of the car!" The salesman left laughing all the way out of the lot. His mechanic was the next to return and Moe knew it was his last chance to get out of the vehicle. Arms being pulled, neck twisting, but no movement. The driver's door had jammed and could not be opened. The mechanic ran around to the passenger side and tried yet again to pull him out - to no avail. Moe could not suck in his stomach as he did to get into the car. He simply squeezed his way down and deep.

The mechanic was not aware that Moe looked as though he was going to die. He thought that his color looked as though it was starving for blood. Out of urgency the mechanic quickly ran to the shop and put a rope around Moe's neck and then beneath each arm to make a harness. He thought that he would get him out the way he got in. Moe was screaming at the mechanic to do something quickly as he was losing his energy. If he had suffered a heart attack he would have had to die in the car, which scared him even more. "Hurry up you stupid fuck. Get me out of here!!" The mechanic threw the rope over a heavy tree limb above and tied it onto the front bumper of his Jeep. He pulled slowly on Moe's body as the tree limb started to sag and Moe started to scream from the excruciating pain. The mechanic ignored the screaming and suddenly, the drivers door popped open. The steering wheel broke, but Big Moe came loose.

The police arrived because anyone driving by would have thought there was a lynching at Big Moe's car lot. The police

Lemon Juice

took Moe to the hospital for tests and an evaluation, while the seller was yelling to Moe "What about my car? You broke the front seat and the door! I can't drive my car because you broke the steering wheel too you fat fuck!" From the rear of the police wagon one could hear Big Moe yelling back: "Fuck you and that fucking little fart of a car!"

Unlike Big Moe, who was driven out of business in 90 days, that first year my partner, Bobby and I netted $90,000 clear profit. Not too bad for my first experience as a professional used car dealer. PS: The average working man's income in 1955 was $5,000 annually.

Subsequently, we handed over the lease to a friend of ours. His parents lent him the money that he would need for inventory, feeling that it was a great investment when they knew how well Bobby and I had been doing. One year later that young man went broke, as did all the dealers prior to us.

Chapter Nine

Northeast Autorama

A black Cadillac limousine pulled up onto our sidewalk in front of Northeast Autorama and parked without regard to being ticketed. A chauffeur dressed in livery opened the rear door while two men exited wearing long black cashmere topcoats to insulate them from the chilly weather. They told us that we could stay up to six months if we signed a contract with them immediately or else no deal. This was puzzling…

Over one year prior I was returning from the seashore on Route 73 after crossing the Tacony-Palmyra Bridge heading to Roosevelt Boulevard on my way home. On my left side at the intersection of Roosevelt Boulevard commonly known as US Highway 1, was a Mobile gas station that had a recent FOR LEASE sign. I quickly jotted down the phone number and as soon as I reached my destination at home, I called the number on the sign. However, being the weekend, there was no response. Monday morning at 8 o'clock I called again. No response. At 8:30am I placed another phone call and received an answering machine that stated the offices would open

Lemon Juice

at 9 o'clock. At exactly 9 o'clock I called yet again and was transferred to their Real Estate department.

I told the person who answered my call that I passed by the location and would like to lease the property, however it was their intent to lease it as a gas station. I told them that I wanted it for a used car sales lot to supplement my existing business on North Broad St. He told me he would need managerial approval for my use and in the meantime he would check out my credit. I told him that no one had better credit than me, but to go ahead and inquire into my credit rating because I knew it was excellent and supplied him with business and personal references. I'm not even a patient patient but told him I would be patient while he evaluated my credit worthiness.

Later that day I called back to the real estate person I had spoken to and wanted to know if he had an answer for me yet. He said he had just walked out of a meeting with his boss and they would gladly do a deal right away. Evidently the gas station wasn't proving to be profitable for Mobile and it wasn't worth putting up with the aggravation that one finds being a landlord.

The rental was only $100 a month more than we were paying at Broad Street Auto Center so I was thrilled! I informed Bobby and he took a ride over to take a look at the location. We discussed the location and what it would need to transform the property into a lucrative used car lot. After giving the pros and cons some consideration, we both gave it the 'thumbs up' even though individually we both knew that we wanted this place.

Northeast Autorama

Less than one week later we had signed the contracts, subject to our getting approval for a used car lot zoning. That would be quite a feat since there was not one used car dealer on Roosevelt Boulevard and zoning was regulated by not just the City of Philadelphia but also input from the Fairmount Park and the Art Commission. Bobby and I placed phone calls to a couple of attorneys that we knew asking their opinion about getting zoning approval. Neither of them laughed at my questions, but their response was basically 'you have to be kidding, no one is going to get permission from the City of Philadelphia, the Fairmount Park and the Art Commission.

We could have simply walked away and received a refund of our deposit, but that's not like me. If there was a way to get this done I would expend every effort possible because I really liked this facility not caring that it was surrounded by Ginko trees which blocked the visibility significantly of this super location. I felt that it could not be duplicated and I wanted to leave Broad Street even though we were one of the most profitable dealers on the entire Broad Street strip.

I placed phone calls to the zoning board asking one of the supervisors *'in his opinion, who was the most successful zoning attorney?'* He told me the same thing that other people in a lesser position had; that he wasn't allowed to recommend an attorney. I stopped him and said *"I'm not asking for a recommendation. I just would like to know who is THE most successful attorney that applies for zoning."* He told me there's an attorney by the name of Irving Stander. I immediately contacted that attorney and informed him what I wanted to do.

Lemon Juice

No one told me at the time however that Irving Stander had written the current zoning codes for the City of Philadelphia. He gave me a list of items that he wanted and immediately sent a professional photographer to take photographs of the existing dingy gas station from all angles and then instructed us to go to City Hall.

We sat in the zoning board hearing room waiting for Irving Stander to arrive. Five minutes - no attorney - 15 minutes no attorney. "Mr. Stander... it's so good to see you," one zoning board member stated, as the other board members all stood up when my lawyer walked in. Not only did they recognize him, but they admired him and he was still very active in the zoning commission well into his 80s. He presented our case and handed to each individual board member a series of photographs. He showed them it would be an upgrade from the gasoline station at that location and he believed every ordinance enacted would provide for this use, even though no other used car facility existed on Roosevelt Boulevard.

Thankfully, the presentation made by this prestigious attorney facilitated the approval almost immediately and unanimously. His $800 legal fee was an absolute bargain! He passed away in 1998 and there is an annual award presented by the Pennsylvania Bar Association in his honor.

One week after receiving the lease signed by the Mobile Oil representatives we were open for business. We expedited through Mobile the decommissioning of the gas tanks, the removal of the islands where the pumps stood. We had signs painted around the top of the building proudly announcing

"**Northeast Autorama.**" We took the front section where the operator had his cash register and a customer seating area and gutted it, quickly turning it into an office. In the rear where the oil drums had been stored, we paneled the walls and framed out a second office behind it. We had several quartzite light poles erected to aluminate our new used car lot.

At the intersection where both streets met, we placed a two-tone Volkswagen minivan on the point for display and purchased enough cars to fill the lot. I don't remember if we even placed any advertisements in the newspaper at that time, but by the end of the week we had cleared $2,750 in profits.

Reflecting back on everything that happened, it was quite amazing! I've seen people that wanted to either lease or purchase a property, but it took so long to get the process completed, that by the time they opened for business a year or more would have passed. That would have driven me crazy.

Over a year or so later, I received a call from someone in the Mobile Oil Corporation real estate department that they were interested in selling the property even though I still had some time left on my lease. I really must have been naïve because I do not remember that we had any type of option for a lease renewal past the first term. The thought never entered my mind since I was just happy to get a lease and open for business. They were asking for the highest bid amount, which got me upset because I wanted an actual dollar amount quoted - not an auction bid. I told them that I will be glad to purchase the property if they would take $55,000 for it, plus take back a mortgage. They seemed extremely receptive to this offer.

Lemon Juice

"*We represent a major shoe company and we are purchasing this property. We want to give you the opportunity to stay six more months.*" What the hell is going on? Both Bobby and I were perplexed. I told the representative that we are purchasing the property and he might as well leave. He was adamant and kept walking around the property with his associate taking photographs and measurements.

It was a cold winter and a week later yet another person came in wearing a long brown heavy top coat. "*My name is Norman Kasser. I'm the owner of Steer-In Restaurants and I am purchasing this property.*" Now what?!! That's not going to happen!! "Noooo, this is my property and I'm not moving," I retorted as I asked Norman to please leave.

I called the representative from Mobile and told him that I needed to know quickly and in writing that we have a contract to purchase this property. Bobby and I had butterflies in our stomachs. It was worse than being in jail for a night. He told me he would get back to me in the morning. It was a long night of waiting. I spoke with him the following morning. He told me to come in to sign the contracts and bring my down payment with me. What a relief I thought! Everything went smoothly in Center City. As we walked out of the door, Norman Kassar still wearing his heavy top coat that was nearly touching the floor and whose family also owned Kasser's Distillery in Philadelphia, came up to me and said "*I'll give you a $35,000 profit for the property.*" I brushed him off and could not wait until we got to **our** property.

Northeast Autorama

As for those two characters who arrived in the black Cadillac limousine wearing the long black cashmere topcoats, they were never heard of again. It seems their intent was to intimidate us into signing a contract with them so they could purchase the property for a shoe store - if that was really their intention.

Our used car lot was located on Highway US, 1, a major highway and was intersected by Levick Street which was the main road that lead from the New Jersey - Pennsylvania and Tacony-Palmyra bridges. You could not ask for more prime location teeming with thousands of motorists passing by daily, plus easy access afforded into our car lot with its many driveways. There was however one drawback, the lot was surrounded by large trees along the entire Route 1 area known as Roosevelt Boulevard.

There, existed the Fairmount Park and Art Commission, which was created for the beautification of the area. To remove a single tree was a crime and to do it legally was proven very difficult, unless the court granted permission to remove trees.

People wanting or needing to remove trees had gone to court to prove a hardship existed. As trees matured they blocked the view from prospective customers, but it was a long process to petition the court and many times these requests were denied because the court would adhere to the park commission's regulations.

Being someone who would always try to improve a situation, I was not content to have these trees surround my property for many reasons, one of which was that Ginko trees shed and

Lemon Juice

were odoriferous. The other reason was those trees blocked the visibility of my property from traffic driving by. Action had to be taken.

I contacted numerous tree companies inquiring as to how I could address this problem. I was told by arborists to drive copper spikes into the base of the tree and then pour gallons of kerosene at the base of the trunk. This was easy but frustrating. We simply walked past each tree with a hammer in hand and started to hammer away. The next day we walked past each of the 12 trees with 5 gallon cans filled with kerosene and poured them as per instructed. We then waited for the results. Days, weeks and months went by. The spring arrived and all the trees that we worked on were the first to display new buds. The grass around them was thick and dark green. So much for those instructions.

I called several tree experts and questioned them about the possibility of removing the trees. These high monster trees had boughs of over 30 inches and seemed to soar up into the clouds. The arborists laughed and told me first that it was illegal to remove trees without having approval, but gave me a price of $150 per tree if for some reason we were able to obtain approval. That gave me second thoughts. But still, something had to be done. Then came Alfonse...

A peg leg Damon Runyon character dressed in baggy pants which were partially dragging on the ground as he limped along wearing a sloppy jacket wrapped around his torso. Alfonse told us that he could have a legitimate tree expert authorized by the Fairmount Park remove all the trees for

$400 but - he would need to block off traffic on US Route 1 so that it would keep costs down and his subcontractor would use a Fairmount Park truck. It was a dark green stake bodied maintenance vehicle that he used on the job. This meant we would lose some business while his crew blocked off the street in order to work, but if he could remove the trees legitimately, then it was worth it in the long run.

He would arrange to have a crew at our location at exactly 4pm. This was the time that the three surrounding police departments had shift changes. The time was perfect because those police did not care what was happening as long as they were not late to work. Those leaving their eight hour shift were heading home in heavy traffic.

I was a bit uncomfortable since I really wasn't totally convinced that Alfonse's tree guy was authorized by the Fairmount Park even though he had credentials and a Fairmount Park maintenance vehicle. I wondered if he was moonlighting to bring in extra bucks, as so many people did, but I had no reason to suspect otherwise. My partner Bobby was less concerned since he spoke with the tree surgeon and felt that he was totally forthright.

I confronted Alfonse and he assured me that he wanted it done at that time so that no one would recognize the tree guy since he was the one moonlighting to make extra money.

The exposure of my used car lot to additional thousands of motorists certainly would mean more business. The job went smoothly. After seeing the first mammoth tree drop to

Lemon Juice

earth and cut up quickly, I was happy but nevertheless still concerned, given my nagging doubts about the validity of Alfonse's guarantee that everything was on the 'up and up.' As the second tree dropped, it seemed as if the sky was opening up. The lot received more light from across this major highway and I could now see my frontage that had not been visible a mere 30 minutes prior. Wow! One, two, three, four and more trees down.

Cars were jammed up as far as the eye could see down the road, as they waited to be directed around this maintenance job. 'What a stupid time to do this type of work,' motorists must have thought. And they would be right, but not for us.

These were the quickest operators I have ever seen. It looked as if it was on a fast-forward motion film. Within one and a half hours, the job was complete and the remaining crew swept up the pavement as the stake bodied trucks drove away.

When I returned from across the highway, the job was finished and my frontage looked super. My used car lot was now fully exposed, I thought.

I still wonder to this day if Alfonse was really working with the Fairmount Park and Art Commission(?)

As I so often felt, if something is not being used to its highest and best use, then action must be taken. The sidewalk in front of Northeast Autorama facing Route 1 was quite wide. I never understood the need for such a wide pavement since very few people ever walked there. Having recently removed many trees which blocked the view of my used car display and having this extra wide sidewalk being there for no apparent reason, was too much for me to take.

Our car lot surface was mostly covered with asphalt and some areas were cement. To make it more uniform I had applied asphalt sealer with a tar base to the entire surface. The perimeter on the lot had steel posts set in the ground and holes cut at the top section through which a thick chain was threaded. This was used to control car thefts which were prevalent. The blacktop sealer stopped at the poles for that is where our car lot met the public sidewalk. On the Levick Street side the sidewalk was very narrow and fully utilized. The Route 1 traffic side needed some of my utmost attention.

While my shop people were applying the asphalt sealer, I tried to stretch my car lot boundaries as far as possible. I thought that I could acquire an additional 10 feet of depth by the entire hundred foot frontage. To do it relatively simple I would remove the post that were in the ground and move them forward by ten feet. I had holes bored into the ground and sunk the posts into their new position. Immediately, I had my crew spread the blacktop sealer as quickly as possible. Instantly, a new frontage was put into use for display, but it presented another problem.

Our sign was a huge 5 feet by 20 feet and had three faces. It stood high in the air. It was an original design made for us by a custom sign company at a cost of $4,500.00 in 1963. However, now the sign appeared to be in the middle of some of our cars on the frontline since we moved our property forward. To

Lemon Juice

correct this and to get the full advantage of this extra land took a couple of weeks to work out. I had placed a telephone call to another sign company to make a template of the three posts, which supported my sign. They would have to bring their own machines and drill three large holes in the ground and forms would have to be made to keep the exact position. The owner of the company wanted $500 in cash, perhaps thinking this job wasn't 'kosher,' still in all he would handle it.

Boring machines were brought to the site along with 12 inch steel posts. The holes were bored. The three posts were set in place and the forms attached to hold the pedestal in place. A load of cement was poured into each hole and steel rods were then placed for added strength. When it was complete, the area was swept clean. The three posts remained in an upright position standing nearly 3 feet above the surface. We slid a compact sports car in between the triangle by the posts. We did not want to look as if something had taken place. Phase 1 was now complete.

Phase 2 took place one week later and went smoothly. A crane was brought to the site and hooked to the top of our existing sign. A welder cut off the top of the sign, which was suspended in mid-air as the rig moved it gently to his new location. Immediately, the welder positioned the cut off poles directly inside the new steel pipes and started welding. As soon as they were finished and the metal cooled off, I sprayed the poles with black paint. At the base where fresh cement had already cured, we covered that with the asphalt sealer. A few minutes later the electric lights were connected and

Northeast Autorama

turned on as the sign company fled the scene with cash in hand. Instant land claim.

A cement contractor from the Hunting Park section of Philadelphia had been doing many jobs for me over the years, including work at Northeast Autorama, where he built numerous brick pillars to highlight a display area. This time I needed him to do some work - quickly. We had success widening our car lot and moving the sign however, around each tree that we removed was a significantly large grassy area. We had him dig out the dirt and grind the stumps below the surface and as fast as he could work, fill the area with stone at the base and cover it with 6 inches of concrete.

Everything was going fine that particular day when a Lieutenant from the Fairmount Park guards drove into our lot. "What is going on here?" He said in a very loud tone. "Do you have permits for this work?" He asked. I looked at him and said "Why are you busting my balls? First we get complaints from the city that we have broken concrete and people could trip. They insisted that we get it repaired immediately or else I will be fined. When are you going to stop harassing me?" The lieutenant apologized and drove off.

From beginning to end over that two-week period, we opened the exposure of our car facility to traffic on the opposite side of the highway that never knew we existed.

Back to business as usual.

Lemon Juice

One thing I recognized was that we needed some unusual advertising because there was a lull in the automobile industry that hit every dealer including us. Customers were concerned about the economy and buying a new or used car was something that they were willing to put off until the economy improved. Dealers had cut back on most of their advertising to preserve cash. I had to do something to drum up business, so I contacted all the television stations that covered the Philadelphia area. This was back in the days way before cable television when the main three stations were CBS, NBC and ABC plus the UHF's. The UHF stood for Ultra High Frequency.

I contacted every TV station and told them I had the desire to overwhelm them with business by purchasing any and all of their unsold airtime at a rate that was far below their lowest 'rate card' ever offered.

I really did not care what time the commercials aired since I certainly could not afford to be on the evening news and I assumed that having more 'spots' would draw more and more attention to Northeast Autorama. I did not care if the commercials aired in the early morning hours or late at night, providing the price was right. Since the economy was in the doldrums, all three of the UHF stations were drooling to accept my proposal as well as one of the national stations.

Now, I had to come up with a personality and a face that was recognizable to represent Northeast Autorama. From one of the national affiliates, I interviewed a well-known sportscaster, who appeared on the evening news daily. He was an impressive

Northeast Autorama

figure entering my office tall and slender wearing a navy blue sport jacket and gray slacks which went well with his gray hair.

Sitting opposite me at my desk I asked him numerous questions and was impressed, however my eyes did not focus on him but kept moving toward the shoulders of his blue sport jacket. It looks like someone had dropped powdered soap flakes on the top of this jacket. He had what appeared to be an uncontrollable dandruff problem. I felt embarrassed that I couldn't look him in the eyes. I just kept looking at the all this unbelievable amount of dandruff on his jacket. I told him that I would get back to him if I was interested. I never called him.

A well known radio disc jockey named Joe Niagara was the next person I interviewed. When he came into my office with his right hand outstretched, sporting an enormous smile, the room reverberated from the energy that I felt within him. He had a great sense of humor and made a nice appearance. However there was one drawback. Joe Niagara had been one of several people who got caught up in the "Payola" scandal. Payola was taking bribes to play certain records. There had been a crackdown by Government officials concerning giving bribes to disc jockeys to gain airtime for certain recorded music.

The law-enforcement officials presented the group who got caught up in this Payola web in the Philadelphia area with a choice. They could all be indicted and face trial - or if one of them admitted to this crime, they would drop the case against the others. As Joe Niagara told me personally, they drew straws. They actually took several matches and the one who

Lemon Juice

had the shortest match would be the one that took the blame and would plead guilty. Joe came up with the short match. All the others had previously agreed that whoever got the short match would be financially compensated by the others who went free. That happened for only a short period time.

I told Joe that if our commercials were successful with the amount of airtime that I was proposing, that he may actually get another job as a disc jockey on a major radio station, since he had been previously blackballed from working on those stations. We agreed and he was willing to accept a low payment per commercial just to get his career back into television.

I started to compose a variety of commercials, each being either 15 seconds, 30 seconds or 60 seconds. I surprised myself that these commercials flowed so effortlessly from me.

Sam Tees, my chauffeur at that time, drove me to the TV studio where we were to perform our first commercials. Since new car dealers were not selling cars at their previous rate, there was a shortage of used cars. I had envisioned Joe Niagara standing alongside the sign for Northeast Autorama telling the public to come to us and receive the most money for their used car.

To make the commercial a little bit different, I was able to get a very high A-frame ladder into the premises of the TV station. Since I always carried hundred dollar bills, I had Sam Tees climb the A-frame ladder out of the view of the TV camera and when Joe Niagara would say that we want to buy your

Northeast Autorama

cars, I told Joe to say 'The sky is the limit!' That was the cue for Sam to drop a flurry of one hundred dollar bills from the ladder onto Joe.

I can still see Joe Niagara with hundred dollar bills that I had pinned onto his lapels looking up in the air as he said 'the sky is the limit' and one of the hundred dollar bills falling from above hitting him directly in the eyeball.

Joe flinched for a second from the impact. Even though we had done this commercial five times, I told Joe that I wanted to go with the one that hit him in the eye as that was the best one.

Now, here's the screwiest part. People were watching these commercial at all hours! They were seeing them at 2am, 3am, 4am, 11pm, no matter what time they aired, we started to get activity immediately!

I was overjoyed - however the activity wasn't people coming to my place to sell their cars, no, it was just the opposite. They came off the bus, which stopped in front of my lot, with their license plates in paper bags to buy cars from me. I was elated!! Now, I really needed cars to the extent that I could go to the auctions and buy cars knowing that I already had customers waiting to buy my cars.

Running so many commercials day and night was an effective tool in bringing activity to my business because it provided a readymade market for sales!

Lemon Juice

Joe Niagara came up with an idea to tag our television advertisement: "At Northeast Autorama, You can't bounce a meatball," which we subsequently painted on our Jeep. He told me that he had watched a comedy skit one time which ended with "You can't bounce a meatball." It was totally meaningless but effective since people wound up asking us 'What does that mean?'

We had previously taken in trade a Jeep with 4 wheel drive, which had an enclosed cab that we used for parts pick up. We painted the Jeep in bright colors and had printed "Northeast Autorama" on the side. I purchased 50 pounds of ground hamburger from a local supermarket. I didn't care if the meat was rancid or not, just give me a good price and plenty of bags to put it in. I had my mechanic Eddie Dye drive the Jeep carrying the meatball to the TV station studio. Now Joe Niagara would have an unusual prop. I had composed plenty of commercials that we would perform impromptu providing we had enough studio time.

Commercials at that time went by the prevailing Union agreement of two commercials per hour. I thought that was crazy because I certainly could fit in more since I was learning how the camera operator was doing his work and how to use the equipment to work the teleprompter.

Now, on the studio set was our Jeep and 50 pounds of hamburger meat shaped into one big meatball sitting on the rear door in front of a pair of hinged doors. On cue when Joe Niagara came close to finishing his commercial and started to say "You can't bounce a meatball at Northeast

Northeast Autorama

Autorama," Eddie Dye would push open the doors and propel the humongous meatball out of the Jeep. The first time that Eddie tried to push the meatball, he fell off balance hitting the studio floor at the same time as the meatball splattered. We did it again and this time Eddie realized the position he had to be in, so that he would not fall onto the studio floor. We did it once again and this time it worked perfectly. No one saw Eddie push the meatball as he laid low on the floor and the meatball dropped with a thud onto the studio floor.

I spent $15,000 that month buying commercial time as low as $2 each. This generated additional income for the TV station, whereas unsold time brought them nothing.

I did not have the money when I signed the contracts and took a chance that I could create activity. Friends of mine in the business asked me if I was crazy to spend all that money when times were so tough. My remark to them was: "There is no debtor's prison."

The commercials were so successful that our business boomed in those bad economic times. We knew the increased business was due to those commercials because customers would invariably ask us: "What does 'You can't bounce a meatball' mean?" The answer is: It meant money in the bank for Northeast Autorama.

With the turnaround of our business we kept plugging away with TV commercials averaging 80 commercials a week. Then suddenly, I was barred from one television station for making 13 commercials myself within a two hour period.

Lemon Juice

The reason I was barred was that according to the Union agreement, only two commercials per hour were permissible. "How could you only air two commercials an hour when you can do for six or eight of them?" I argued to no avail. I started to produce commercials at one of their competitors.

I was so comfortable doing these commercials with Joe Niagara, that we kept bringing in customers to appear in testimonials.

A newspaper article was written about Northeast Autorama and at the conclusion, the reporter believed that Joe Niagara actually owned Northeast Autorama.

Over a year later Joe Niagara became as recognized as he was when he had been on the air prior to the Payola scandal. Then, a major radio station offered him a job. I was thrilled that Joe was on the air again being a disc jockey and my business was booming.

Eventually, Joe Niagara was inducted into the Rock and Roll Hall of Fame and his star was placed on the "Walk of Stars" in Philadelphia. You know what they say, you can't bounce a meatball at Northeast Autorama. Apparently, it was very true.

The unique advertising helped bring in customers and our business at Northeast Autorama was constantly growing with a large repeat customer base. Our marketing program giving free lifetime service that included oil changes and filters, lubrication and unlimited complete tune ups had paid off. Parents would bring their children. Workers would bring their fellow employees. It kept our heads above water during market downturns that affected all car dealers.

It helped that I did not know how to relax. I thought about it but relaxing seems to be so unproductive. What do you do when you relax anyway? Simply close your eyes? Lay in a lounge chair? I know people can do that for hours on end, but I just didn't know how to relax at my age.

My wife tried to convince me I should take some time off from work and do something with our children. I heeded her advice but things didn't go as planned.

It was a warm and sunny Wednesday at the National Auto Dealers auction when I was bidding on vehicles in the truck lane. The Chevrolet van that was fitted out with beds and a dining area had just caught my eye. I had an interest in obtaining properties in northwest Pennsylvania and this mini-motorhome seemed to be something that I could have fun with besides making money on it when I had my fill. The bidding was brisk for this almost new van. I was the successful bidder paying $5,500 for it. A good buy. The next day I had plans for the coming weekend. Marlene and I would take the kids camping while I looked to purchase some raw farmland in Potter County, Pennsylvania.

Saturday morning we packed up and waved goodbye to our home feeling the excitement in our systems that so many campers had told us about. The van had all the creature comforts with automatic transmission, power steering and power brakes, especially cool comforting air conditioning.

Lemon Juice

We took the turnpike to the northeast extension passing the Pocono Mountains, still heading north. My plan was to look at some parcels of land, first in the Towanda region, then we would proceed west to the Potter County area where I had already acquired some land. What I did not plan for was simply where to stay. After all, I was in a motorhome so I could stay anywhere I wanted, or so I thought. Nope, not so.

I heard about trailer and camping areas and I had envisioned them as being cute, clean and very rustic. Rustic they were. Cute & clean - not so much. They were filthy with debris and overcrowded. Shit! This is not the Jewish way. I should have realized that those friends who told me about the wonderful world of camping were not Jewish.

Well, there I was, sitting alongside the campground contemplating whether to go home or stay there. After discovering that the van had no electricity of its own, I would not be able to go it on my own. Once again stay or leave? The kids were tired and so was I. I had logged in some seven hours of driving and was weary. I opened the section above the dinette which was a sleeping area for two. That's how the brochure described it. "A full sleeper for four." Two up and two down. The two down accommodations for sleeping was accomplished by resetting the dinette into a mini-bed and the two above in the pop-up section. The two above was to be for our children.

Wanting the children to rest, I opened up the 'second floor accommodations.' It was like opening a panel of a drawer. The opening for the bed area at the ceiling was accessed

Northeast Autorama

through a ladder that was fitted into the bed. However, the opening was only 24 inches in height at the top, a rather narrow space to squeeze into. It would have been extremely uncomfortable for a child to fit in there, let alone an adult. 'Did Christian children get smaller at night while Jews stayed the same size?' was going through my head. How does anyone get into such a small space? Being inventive did not help. The only way we could get small children into that compact space was to grease up their heads with Vaseline and force them into this tight area. Since my kids were not doing anything wrong I decided not to force them into this constricted space. I opened the dinette and setup the blankets on the tables, which we brought with us. The kids rested and got a few winks while I turned the van around and headed for home.

Being filled up with sodas on the way home, the kids used the toilet in the camper many times. It worked, after all it was brand-new. About halfway home the van started to smell. The odor was sickening. From some other uses the toilet holding tank could not hold any more waste. That is where the smell came from. All our other reliefs were made at restaurants along the highway.

At about 1:30 in the morning I pulled into our driveway. Home never looked so good. The following morning the van was cleaned out and placed for sale. I had positioned it in the best spot for our special vehicles, directly under our marquee sign on the corner of Roosevelt Boulevard and Levick Street.

A few days went by and we had our first bite. A man in his 50s wanted a minivan to tour the country. He must have been crazy.

Lemon Juice

Why the hell would anyone familiar with all these discomforts want to punish themselves? The day was as bright and sunny as those before, however the temperatures had risen to the low 90s. My salesman got the keys and opened the sliding door for our potential customer. As he opened the door, the customer started to enter the van placing his right foot on the running board and as he was ready to swing into the camper, he jumped back falling onto my salesman. They both bolted away from the van at the speed of light. Everyone on the lot rushed over to see what happened. Before getting close to the van we all knew. The most nauseating stench had surrounded the van and the closer one attempted to get, the stronger the stink got. Without too much guessing I realize the holding tank must of had all that it could hold and the heat wave was cooking the contents even more. I summoned my porter to get inside and open all the windows. I called some motor home dealers to find out how to get rid of the contents of the holding tank.

A Chevrolet dealership on Street Road was the nearest dealer that had a pumping service. They were nearly 20 miles away and wanted $25 to pump it out. When I asked if there were any special tools needed to empty the holding tank, the man laughed. He told me that one of the side pipes under the van was simply hooked up to their tank and then the lever under the toilet gets pulled. Gravity empties the tank, not suction. I felt $25 was a high price to pay just to let gravity do its job. That's when I decided to try it my way. It was cheaper did not require a 50 mile round-trip and wasted time. I summoned my porter to put a dealer tag on the van, remain in the rear van section while I drove north on Route 1. I had both my side view mirrors adjusted so that I would be able to see cars approaching. When I attained the speed of 55 miles an hour and saw no cars in my area, I told the porter to open the valve. "What?" he responded." "Pull the damn valve - the toilet release," I yelled.

Within a second the holding tank was emptied. Fifty miles and $25 saved in **one minute!** I stopped at a traffic light at Harbison Avenue to make a right-hand turn to head back, when I had a wider view in my rearview mirror. It turned out there **was** a car directly behind the van when the holding tank valve was released. The car was splattered with crap across the hood and windshield. The driver turned on the windshield wipers, which only made matters worse. I pressed the gas pedal to the floor and raced back to the safety of my car lot.

Three hours later I stopped at the same intersection on my way home driving my new 1967 Lincoln Continental cranberry red, four door convertible with the top-down. The sun was shining through the beautiful trees on the boulevard. However, the fecal smell still lingered in the air like the contents of a cesspool. Everything was glorious as long as I didn't have to breathe.

A few weeks later my French poodle, Pierre, and I would walk from our home on Pembroke Avenue in Margate, New Jersey, one block to the marina where my boat 'My Marlene' was tied securely in the boat slip waiting patiently for me to return.

Lemon Juice

At 7 o'clock that morning there was a light fog covering the area that drifted in from the ocean. I could see the sun trying its best to brighten the day and lift the fog. Pierre was anxious to get on board. I helped him to get in and he positioned himself right behind the driver seat. I readjusted my bathing suit and stuffed $5,000 in hundred dollar bills into the right side of my bathing suit as I started the Chrysler straight-eight engine with downdraft carburetors. It was a pleasant roar that the engine and exhaust gave off. I dropped the lines and backed out of the boat slip.

My wife, Marlene, was back home feeling somewhat queasy, as she was pregnant with our son-to-be, Robert. I knew the backwaters pretty well but also had a small map on board for the Jersey Coast with its back channels and waterways. Now, you might be asking what was I going to do going with my dog Pierre and I in a bathing suit with $5,000 stuffed into it? That would be a normal question and here's the answer: I was getting bored and feeling unproductive, which happens every time that I try to relax. How could I be taking off for three months and have my partner Bobby running a business? I never equated my abilities versus Bobby's. When I would return from my summer vacation he could take his. Now getting back to the $5,000. I headed the boat out through the back bay and through the breakwaters to the ocean. On some days this could be a handful but that morning there were just swells gently rolling in and about 5 foot waves. I made a right-hand turn and headed to Ocean City, New Jersey.

Northeast Autorama

I pulled into a public marina, told the dock master that I'd be back in an hour or two, which was my plan. Helping Pierre out of the boat and seeing that the boat was secured, we both walked about a half a mile to the Oldsmobile dealer's facility to speak to their wholesaler.

He was there bright and early and looked at me very quizzically. Who is this guy in a bathing suit and sandals with a dog alongside having no leash? I told him that Jimmy Rappaport is a car merchandiser of mine who has purchased numerous automobiles from his dealership on Jimmy's monthly trips to Ocean City. He then knew who I was. He thought I had looked familiar and then suddenly realized that I was the person he had seen in the past at the car auctions. But this time without a fancy suit and my traditional antique walking stick with a gold handle. I purchased three cars from him, then called Bobby to send some drivers to pick up the automobiles.

Leaving their Oldsmobile dealership, both Pierre and I walked to 12th Street and Asbury to Druck Cadillac-Pontiac, where I met with the accountant who was a partner in the dealerships and handled disposing of the used cars that came in for trade. One-half hour later, having also arranged to have two cars picked up, my sidekick Pierre and I went back to the marina, handed the attendant a $3.00 tip and headed back to Margate.

Two days after the automobiles arrived at Northeast Autorama, the cars were detailed and sold, bringing in $4,000 in cleared profits. I'd have to admit, for someone who was '*relaxing,*' I was

Lemon Juice

rather productive and profitable. But that was not enough - I wanted to do even more.

Anyone that was familiar with me in the automobile business knew no one worked quicker, harder, was more dedicated and above all always honored my word. However, there was a drawback to me always seeking perfection. I would get frustrated with personnel that did not do what they were instructed to do and covered it over with some kind of bullshit lie. It's one thing if someone did not do their job correctly because I would simply asked them to do it again and get it right this time. I never said 'you cost me money and you have to pay to do something over with my mechanics or detail people.' I would be furious if a sales person told me that they contacted a customer when they did not. I've always had a feeling down the back of my spine when someone was lying to me. I could tell before words came out of their mouth that a lie was on the way out of their mouth. It put me at an advantage when they were selling something because I could filter through the feedback that I was getting and knew how to close a deal.

Eddie Dye was an all-around mechanic who would do anything you wanted. He was pleasant to be around and there simply was nothing that he would not do if I asked. In the shop that was adjacent to my office, he had a stack of window panes 22"x28". They were the size of the windowpanes in the bow windows around my office and the office on the other side of the shop. Why you ask would he have a stack of window panes? Well, the reason was…

Northeast Autorama

I got off the phone in my rear office and walked to the front area where the salesmen sat. *"Who's that customer on the frontline?"* I asked my salesman. *"Oh, he's no one. Just was walking around the street."* No way was I going to believe that. I put on my jacket because it was a little chilly as fall was here with the leaves looking gorgeous on the trees across the street and on the perimeter of our lot. I walked out the front and spoke with this person just passing by. I asked him what car he was interested in and he walked me a few spaces to where we had a 1961 Oldsmobile four-door in a beautiful powder blue. It was a super nice car that I used the previous summer going up and back to the shore. Thirty minutes later Eddie was placing temporary tags on the rear bumper and we made a handsome profit.

"Crash!" That was the sound of my foot going through the window pane closest to my salesman, Warren. We used to call him LOS for "Load Of Shit." Warren was six foot two and a good 275 pounds, who had a problem telling the truth about anything. Warren had a great affinity to strike up conversations with a potential customer and they looked upon him as a friend. That's the only reason that we didn't fire him, but now it was a different story. *"You lying piece of shit. You cannot tell the truth about anything and there's $100 commission you're going to get and you didn't do anything except lie!"* That's when I put my foot through the window pane. At the sound of the crashing glass, Eddie appeared with a small putty knife and a very light weight upholsterer's hammer and one pane of glass 22"x28". *"The glass is changed, Gene,"* he said satisfied with his repair job.

Lemon Juice

Once a week Eddie would be right on top of things with a dustpan and broom ready to sweep up shards of glass after I blew off steam. Now I understood why he keep so much glass in stock.

Eddie would have yet another job to do that week. One of our repeat customers, Milt and his friend "Brother John" would stop in every couple weeks simply to chat and maybe go to Horn and Hardart restaurant next door to get a bite to eat with us. Brother John was deep into the Muslim religion and would explain things about it to us. Over the years, the two of them must have purchased six or seven automobiles and gave us plenty of recommendations. And those customers brought us even more business.

Milt called me one day in the middle of the week and asked if I wanted to attend the Mohammad Ali fight at Madison Square Garden in New York. That weekend Bobby and I were seated with Milt and Brother John surrounded by a host of black people. Bobby and I appeared to be only two white pimples in contrast to the group around us. I had plenty of things going on in my mind and did not pay much attention to the fight except that I recall Mohammad Ali won the boxing match rather quickly.

One of Milt and Brother John's recommended customers purchased a '58 Chrysler New Yorker convertible that was dark green with a black convertible top and black leather interior. It was in perfect condition. The customer gave us a one-third down payment in cash and we were financing the balance. He thanked everybody and left - only to return a few

Northeast Autorama

days later demanding the title, even though he owed us the balance. We obviously refused. No dealer turns over the title until a car has been paid in full. We tried to explain this to him, but he refused to listen.

He told us that he was a "Black Panther" [a *militant group*] and he will have our place burned down if we didn't give him the title to the car. Barton (Bart) Goldsmith was our manager who had sold the automobile to him. He was the key person to whom customers would refer other customers.

There were customers in the front office so Bart told the future arsonist to go into my private office to discuss this matter. There was Bart, who was about 5 foot 8 inches tall and weighed 225 pounds, telling this militant that it was required for him to pay the outstanding balance we had agreed upon and had a signed contract, before we could turn over the title to him.

The guy didn't seem to grasp the legalities of obtaining a title only AFTER paying the remaining balance owed. He got exceedingly angry and took a swing at Bart. I saw this happen in an instant and was shocked. Bart then went nose to nose with this guy and before you knew it, they were grappling on the floor swinging at each other as Bobby and I stood there traumatized.

They rolled into an 80 gallon fish tank filled with tropical fish as they tussled with one another. Bobby ran over to keep the tank from falling off its foundation. I ran into my closet and pulled out a .22 caliber air rifle that had a somewhat realistic

Lemon Juice

look. Bart had reached behind this militant fellow and had both of his hands under this guy's armpits, holding him over Bart's body with his chest facing the ceiling. Bart yelled "Kill the son of a bitch!" I pointed the rifle at my customer's face and softly said "I know you're going to pay the balance as agreed, since I want you to give the payments directly to Brother John — and never, ever return to this place." As the customer left, Eddie came in to clean up the few gallons of water that had spilled onto the floor from the tank, as it was being rocked back and forth during the flight. It's a good thing we had Eddie to mop up after altercations because he came in quite handy over the years.

In 1962, we took in trade a 1954 Oldsmobile Holiday two-door coupe with very low mileage. It was black with red leather interior and silver-gray inserts. I liked the style of the car and for a while I made it my 'driver' using it daily. My daughter Ellen was just almost two years old at the time and I put the baby seat on the passenger side backrest as everyone did. I don't remember where we were going at the time, however I vividly remember hitting the brakes rapidly to avoid someone who just ran a traffic light.

As the car came near a halt I quickly put my right arm out to stop the passengers back rest holding my daughter from hitting the dashboard. That night I sketched drawings of the first seat lock mechanism. It was a simple two-piece device with a male end on one side and a female receptor. To install them you would simply use a Phillips screwdriver to remove the hard plastic stops that met each other when the seat was in an upright position. A ball bearing would be spring-loaded to lock the assembly. To unlock it a T handle would be depressed from the side of the seat releasing the ball bearing and leaning the seat forward. My intentions were to have these mass-produced and sell them to national automotive stores at that time with Pep Boys in mind.

An attorney by the name of Paul from a law firm in Center City, Philadelphia looked over the sketches along with an engineer and both were definitely negative in their opinion on this being successful. Me, being 22 or 23 years old thought that the lawyer knew was his talking about. He told me to buy TWA stock which was $86.25 at the time, instead of spending $800 on having my item patented.

He passed away not too long after that meeting.

I held onto my TWA stock for years. It never went to the $86.25 again in its history and I sold it at $6 a share. At that point I stopped taking business advice from lawyers.

After one accountant tried to extort $6,000 from me and a top lawyer in the City of Philadelphia who represented me, which I discovered later was working in concert with my partner to my financial disadvantage, I sort of lost faith in our system. It was a couple of years later that seat lock mechanisms were introduced and subsequently became mandatory globally.

Back in the 1950s there was a person named Ann Hastings who for $6.00 would search patent records in Washington, DC for ideas that potential customers had. I compare that to

Lemon Juice

advertisements you see on television quite often for companies that will handle your patent applications.

My mother first sent her idea about a woman's brassiere with a zipper in the front. That was very novel. Another idea of hers was for pre-sweetened teabags or with dehydrated lemon. Not too long after that Maidenform came out with a brassiere with a closure in the front. And Lipton came out with a teabag similar to my mother's idea.

Chapter Ten

Estate Liquidators

In 1967, a huge 20,000 square foot building became available for sale in my old neighborhood. Knowing that recently dealers were selling cars from garages and doing well, I decided that my partner and I should not miss this opportunity. It was the old Miller North Broad Street storage garage and it was available for $60,000. I never found out why it was called Miller N. Broad Street because it was on Albanus Street; a street so small that I don't think anyone even in close proximity would have ever heard of it.

It ran a short distance and had terrible access. Later, I was to use a nonexistent address: 4941 Old York Road, which would be close enough to the building that if you walked toward number 4941, you would see a sign directing you to our company The cost of $60,000 for this building was fair enough, however it was in need of a multitude of repairs. The area was roughly 100'x200' and would be able to accommodate nearly 70 automobiles on the interior.

Lemon Juice

The place was dingy, the roof leaked in several places. The ceiling beams were full of rust flakes, the brick walls were spewing out chalk between the layers. The floor was full of grease. It smelled like a pit in which mechanics of a bygone era would drive the cars onto ramps. Even so, it was perfect for what I had envisioned I would do with this building; a place where you would expect vehicles belonging to a funeral home to be stored. A neat, clean and thoroughly organized facility where flower-cars would be adorned.

To accomplish this, the most important item needed was **money**. My partner and I could not raise all the money that was required, so we needed to rely on banks to fund us. Not good. It was a time when mortgage money was tight. It seemed as though all of my life when I needed money it was at a time when mortgage money was tight. 'Tight' meant no money, no matter what.

The only answer was to get another partner. This brought about Tony Davis. He was once a competitor of mine, who sold his share of a business and decided to semi-retire. After a short time he went into a business with Stanley Friedburg.

Stanley was a tyrant and impossible to deal with. After Stanley grabbed Tony by the throat and threatened to smash his head against the wall for disliking the cars that he was buying, Tony decided to break up the partnership before **he** was broken into tiny pieces by Stan.

Tony, as I got to know him better, was a 'downer,' his favorite cliché being: "Let's paint the blackest picture possible." I could not take hearing that all the time. I was ready to call Stan to finish Tony off.

Tony took so long making a decision that neither of us could stand it. Out of desperation we called my brother Mickey and his partner in the used car business, Pete. Between the four of us we could amass the money needed for the building and the contemplated improvements. We all clicked very well. They were hustlers and so were we. It was a shame to split the bounty between all of us, but we could not obtain a mortgage no matter how hard we tried. We consummated a deal and within a week we had it on paper.

Contractors were called for estimates. Those who never showed were lucky because they were not put through having to deal with either one of us - or possibly all of us together. We promised them all the jobs in the future and I explained how this would be our premier job and they would be the sole painters, carpenters on all our projects opening soon. However, their price must be extra reasonable because this was **our** money, not future money coming in from investors. That was pretty true.

We designed a Cape Cod one-story edifice with four comfortable offices and one larger master office. It would have been too difficult for my partners to accept my office as the largest, so the extra large office would accommodate two huge desks with several side chairs for customers and guests. It also had an extremely comfortable sofa and a solid mahogany credenza, refrigerator as well as a liquor cabinet.

Lemon Juice

Attached to this office was a huge bathroom with an extra large shower and toilet. It was to service four people at once. Never to hurt either one's feelings, there was a private entrance which had an electric lock so the door could only be opened by pressing one of several buttons located in our offices. The other access was through our adjacent secretarial office.

The exterior finish was clapboard being traditional Cape Cod with the siding in a barn red with white wood trim. There was an overhang to protect the rain which was appropriate with a Cape Cod design, however there was no rain since this building was indoors. We saved money by not needing a real roof. The ceiling was a facade. We wanted our offices to be different and this was our primary step.

The ceiling contractors sealed the holes and scraped the flaky particles from the ceiling and the beams. The painter sprayed the ceiling white, then trimmed the beams and metal structures in aluminum paint finish. When this was done, the building looked fresh, at least when you looked up. It's certainly lit up the previously dingy building.

The walls were pressure cleaned and the bricks painted again in white, replacing bricks were limited to those that really were most urgently needed. The old windows which had hundreds of broken panes of glass where the metal frames were rotted, was cheaper, quicker and more attractive to eliminate the entire 12'x12' frames and replace them with modern new wooden double hung frames.

Estate Liquidators

The electricians were working on scaffolds, as the floor was being etched with an acid wash to prepare for painting.

Roofers were working speedily. Carpenters were installing windows. Masons and cement contractors were repairing the broken sidewalk. Workmen were laying out a small three-car shop for minor mechanical repairs but specifically for complete automobile detailing. Simultaneously, construction was being performed on our office building.

We bounced around many ideas to name our enterprise. I chose: '**Estate Liquidators, Incorporated**." This would, by the sound of it, give the impression that we were not an ordinary car dealer, but disposers of cherished property.

A podium was purchased which would be positioned at our entrance along with a traditional book placed open for signing by visitors, as if it were a funeral people were attending. Ironically, it could have led to some funerals. When everything was complete it was an incredible transition from the old and dingy building to a clean, classy, neatly organized building that housed beautifully detailed automobiles. Every salesman was required to wear a gray suit with a white shirt and a black tie. These were our 'pallbearers,' who would escort the 'mourners' into the confines of our offices, where they would peacefully purchase automobiles.

I felt like a movie director. It was akin to 'The Sting' where a broken down building was miraculously transformed into a gaming establishment. Indeed, it was like that. People were

Lemon Juice

being psychologically set up by programming and vision. The scene was set.

A customer reads the following advertisement in the newspaper classified section: "*1956 Mercury four-door. Kept in splendid condition by past owner and driven only 21,000 miles. Cherished throughout. Equipped with auto, power steering and air conditioning. Must be sold by the Estate Liquidators: $51 a month.*"

This advertisement could be taken in only one way. Someone who cherished their car obviously had passed away and had never contemplated the sale. It was always perfectly maintained. Must have been owned by an elderly person. And the family would be glad to finance it or the banker for the estate.

We had a concrete floor painted a light gray with the car spaces striped in white. Each space was numbered. All cars set in place. A bible looking book spread opened on the podium at the entrance. A poster placed on an easel stating the following: "Thank you for visiting Estate Liquidators, where the finest vehicles have been chosen for your inspection. Please sign the logbook to identify yourself. If you have been sent here by a member of the family, please indicate on the space provided. A representative will show you around. Thank you."

The offices were filled with salesmen who had been briefed on the attitude and aura which we were trying to present. It lasted only a few minutes with most of them for when they had made a sale at a huge profit, they became themselves once more.

Estate Liquidators

In came customer after customer, the phones had been ringing constantly that first morning that we were open for business. Would it work? I was certain it would. "How do you do?" Remarked, my salesman who would say: "I think we have the car that you want." The customer filled out the logbook which was a super way for our managers to follow-up on any sales that we were unable to close that day. The customer was shown around the building, which amazed him. No dirty used car lot. No lightbulbs on strings hanging haphazardly above one's head, which was reminiscent of all used car dealers. This was an immaculate building which housed beautiful new offices in a new building. We had a 'classy joint.' Was that something Jackie Gleason would say?

Finding an automobile which aroused interest in the classified advertisement section of the Philadelphia Inquirer was easy. A customer would never have expected to see an auto so clean. Under the hood was a true work of art. Our engineers were instructed to make the engine compartment look as new as if it had just arrived from the factory. It took them nearly a full day's work - but it was worth it.

The compartment was first degreased of all foreign materials. The valve covers were removed, sanded, primed, and repainted in its original colors. Worn engine decals were replaced with new ones. The hoses were scrubbed or changed, if necessary. The carpeting was also made to look like new. Each area was masked off so that the individual pieces of equipment could be refinished like new. It was a masterpiece which was always shown to a prospective customer.

Lemon Juice

Next to the interior, which had already been vacuumed, scrubbed and dyed if necessary, the rugs were made to look like new. The ashtray was restored inside so it appeared that no one ever sat on the seats, let alone ever smoked a cigarette or cigar.

The exterior was spotless. Each car had been hand custom striped by a fine craftsman, Pete, who often would be at our showroom and to avoid confusion with my partner Pete, I called him "Re-Pete," who was nearing 70 years of age. Re-Pete told stories of hand-striping carriage wheels in his fathers shop. Every scratch was then touched up by this artisan.

The entire picture was magnificent. Nothing to distract a true buyer's interest. Then came the price. Almost too intimidated to ask how much the car cost, when the customer was told the price, they were almost too embarrassed to quibble. Always within view was a handsome heavenly black funeral car which appeared to be waiting for another service. The funeral car was actually fun to take to New York City, which we all used as a limousine on the weekends.

Chapter Eleven

Bored of Education

Frank Rizzo was the new 'law and order' Mayor of Philadelphia. I met him at a social event and really liked him. He was as down-to-earth as you can find in a person, which was not the face of his public persona.

I subsequently sold a car to one of his drivers. I learned that the technical schools in the city had very little access to automobiles for their vocational shop students. I called the office of the Board of Education and offered to donate as many cars as they needed for their automotive teaching facilities, as I took cars in trade. My idea was that the auto body technical school could tear apart these bodies and have the students work on them. Not book learning but simply hands-on education.

The mechanical shop could be pulling out engines and transmissions and teaching electrical and brake work. The schools had nothing to lose for no matter how bad the cars may turn out to be, the students would be learning firsthand, which would give them the experience they needed to apply for better jobs in the future.

At that time we had traded two automobiles that were of no significant value to us since we would not spend the money necessary to fix them for sale. We would simply wholesale them. Instead, we donated them to the vo-tech schools. Within a year, a total of 30 automobiles were donated and I was subsequently offered a seat on the Advisory Council for the Board of Education Technical School.

There was no way that I would have a seat on the council and simply attend meetings. If I was going to take the time, I was going to give them my energy as well. I met with numerous teachers and presented a program that I designed along the lines of the automobile shops. I wanted to teach students masonry, carpentry electrical, plumbing and HVAC.

Again, I wanted the students to have hands-on experience so that they could learn a trade. My concept was to have the shop teachers go into a poor North Philadelphia neighborhood and start at house number one. I would donate $800 at that time to cover parts for plumbing, electrical and carpentry materials. I worked on this program for about a month and found great enthusiasm amongst the teachers. They thought it was wonderful to have children being supervised while learning a trade and simultaneously improving their own neighborhoods.

I received one of my greatest disappointments when I was met with a brick wall in that the Union was worried I would be taking jobs and they would use their pressure to make

Bored of Education

sure this would not come to fruition. I called everyone that I could to no avail. I spoke to a few representatives and told them that there is no way these poor people living in such substandard housing that had cardboard covering broken glass windows, could ever afford to pay $8.00 an hour, which was the prevailing Union wage at that time. Everybody agreed with me, but due to politics, nothing happened. Not one house would they touch.

I had given the speech about my program in front of the Board of Education on the Parkway in Philadelphia. I told them, including representatives of Sun Oil Company and Philadelphia Electric (PECO), that they were all a bunch of hypocrites who attended meetings simply to say that they cared, when in fact "you sit on your ass doing nothing to help the students. You say that you're here as a civic service. That is bullshit!" I looked around and saw faces in shock. I didn't give a damn. I spoke my piece. If they weren't going to help other people in need, then I would do it myself.

In 1978 I received a call from my wife Marlene who sounded very excited "You have to come home now! Stop what you're doing and come home!! You must meet Donald Griffin. He is absolutely the sweetest person I have ever met and I know you will love him. Besides, he has a pair of gorgeous carriage lamps that he wants to sell." I responded: "Let me finish off this one transaction and I'll be right there." I really wasn't excited to meet Donald Griffin, whoever he was, but I'll take a 25 mile drive to purchase a beautiful pair of carriage lamps since I

Lemon Juice

was building up my collection of horse-drawn carriages and accoutrements.

Within an hour I was at our farm and met with Donald W. Griffin, a retired colonel from the US Army Air Force, whose bronze statue is displayed handsomely at his alma mater, Princeton University. As usual, Marlene was right. Upon meeting him and speaking to him he was an absolutely wonderful person. Standing over 6 feet tall with a trim build, he extended his hand for a firm handshake. I don't even remember purchasing the carriage lamps he had for sale, but he told me that years ago he was given a horse-drawn Victoria carriage that could be pulled by either a single horse or a pair. The carriage was in good, solid condition and said he would like to sell it. Originally, the carriage had belonged to the White family who were in the same business as the Singer Sewing machine company and subsequently donated the carriage to Princeton University.

Before I realized it, a few hours had passed and I did not place one telephone call to my car business. That was really rare for even on vacations laying around a swimming pool I always requested an extension telephone cord so that I could be in constant contact with my employees. Obviously, that was in the days before cell phones. What a boon to modern science this invention was!

Donald showed me the carriage at his son's estate in Hopewell, New Jersey. It was everything he described. He was willing to sell it on one condition: I would have to make the carriage available when any of his children or grandchildren got married. I agreed and made the deal. A week later Donald called and

Bored of Education

wanted Marlene and me to join him as his guest for lunch at the restaurant in Princeton University. We had a lovely lunch but more than anything we struck up a wonderful relationship. One day Donald surprised me and showed up at my used car lot in Bordentown, New Jersey.

This time I took Donald to lunch. As our friendship grew, I confided in him the tossing and turning that goes on my mind when I'm doing something to help other people that winds up getting publicity. I told Donald that I don't know if I'm doing something good for people in need strictly to get the publicity. I told him that people always say the greatest gift is one given anonymously. He totally disputed that statement and then asked me: *"When you're doing something good and changing someone's life for the better, who gets hurt if you get publicity for it? If you do get publicity for your charitable work, you would probably make more money - and knowing you - the more money you make - the more you would want to giveaway to help others. By getting publicity, you are setting an example for others to follow. But when it's done anonymously, there is no person to lead the way."*

Over the years the more that I thought about what Donald had said, the more it resonated within me. I kept thinking about what I could do to help more people. Thoughts just popped up out of nowhere and then I found myself wanting to do additional things to help more people. It compelled me to use part of my business income to pay for these philanthropic endeavors and then form a charitable foundation that would work solely to help those that are in the most dire need. One

Lemon Juice

thing I thought we could do was to host a turkey giveaway on Christmas for the homeless. It was such a success, that Marlene and I started doing it on an annual basis.

One Christmas Day in 1980 stands out in my mind because Marlene and I were on our way to our annual turkey giveaway for the indigent. Anyone who was unemployed, on Welfare or receiving Social Security Supplemental Income (SSI) would qualify.

We were driving down route 206 in Hamilton Township, New Jersey, expecting to pass a former gas station that I owned and leased out to Safelite Auto Glass. However, as we were within one block of that location, the police were routing traffic away from that block. You could hear the sounds of fire engines seemingly coming from every direction heading to S. Broad Street and Park Avenue. Just a half-hour before, an explosion occurred while crews from a gas and electric company were working in that area. The explosion damaged my property and the one adjacent to it. I could not get to my property and continued being rerouted until I finally arrived at my used car facility in Bordentown, NJ. Three hundred live turkeys were filling up two of my offices. Complete chaos!

Thoughts kept running through my head that just moments ago I lost a national tenant and the income I needed to fund these charitable events. Then there would be the aggravation of having to put up a new building. But I had to put that incident aside in my mind because people were lined up for over hundred feet waiting as each one presented identification

Bored of Education

to show they met our minimum requirements for my turkey giveaway.

I personally shook hands with each and every person wishing them a Merry Christmas. I was taken aback when a few of them told me of their personal hardships. My building had just blown-up and I faced a long road ahead with contractors, insurance companies and township approvals - but none of it made any difference to me after hearing the individual hardships that these people, waiting for their free turkeys and coupons for food, faced on a daily basis.

Over the course of 35 years, we hosted our turkey giveaway virtually annually, not at my car business anymore, but in synagogues and churches, many times hosting it for Thanksgiving and then Christmas.

One year at Temple Shalom synagogue in Bristol, Pennsylvania, I convinced the rabbi and the board members to have a Christmas party in their synagogue. I forgot to mention that Christmas and Hanukkah fell on the same date that year. I was surprised at how quickly they agreed and wanted to know how many people I needed to help. Initially, I wanted to give away a few hundred turkeys and food coupons because I felt that I had a decent year in business, so I wanted to do something that made a positive difference in these peoples lives.

At Bucks County Community College, they had a business program called SIFE: Students in Free Enterprise, sponsored by Sam Walton from Walmart. I got involved with them, leading discussions in class about entrepreneurship. Later, developing

Lemon Juice

for them my Wheelz2Work program that to date has provided over 450 cars to those needing transportation to get to a new job or additional education, when they could not afford to purchase any type of reasonably priced vehicles. This program won First Place at the national competition for 90 colleges across the country participating in SIFE. I called Professor Joan Weiss, who led this particular group and requested some student volunteers to help put my Christmas party together at Temple Shalom.

The Red Cross homeless shelter was sending 80 people for our turkey and food coupons Christmas party. I had the students solicit companies locally to donate everything they possibly could that we would give away as gifts. The students found it difficult to solicit money, even for a good cause, but they learned how to ask.

I requested that they get a list from the 80 people we knew were coming from the shelter so that we could purchase appropriate gifts, knowing peoples age and gender would greatly personalize each gift. Before long, other organizations that heard about my turkey dinner event were calling to let us know that they had some people to send over too. Over one dozen volunteers from the synagogue were setting up to serve hot turkey dinners, which were homemade and those 80 people soon ballooned up to over 200 guests.

We received a moderate amount of donations, so I proceeded to give my credit card to a couple of the students to make sure that we had enough gifts for everyone. We bought a total of 600 gifts to give out and in the auditorium we had displayed

Bored of Education

a one-horse sleigh from my collection, loaded with gifts in and around the sleigh, covering the entire floor. We gave out tickets for door prizes to all of our guests and I took the role of 'Master of Ceremonies.'

The building shook from the excitement that permeated the entire synagogue and probably traffic passing by could hear people shouting for joy. People that wake up everyday with nothing positive to look forward to, knowing that for one reason or another hardships are their way of life, finally had something positive to look forward to. This night however, would be a night unlike others. Each of our guests were showered with gifts. Each one had a delicious meal like they had never experienced before. The event lasted several hours and culminated with door prizes. The principal prize was a color TV set which added further elation to the event.

That night neither Marlene nor I could sleep, as the adrenaline from the day's events were pumping through our veins like electric thunderbolts. We could not get over all the happiness that we observed that day - but - the shame of it was - it was only for that **one** day. I just knew in my heart I had to do even more.

By 1980, I was donating half of my income to disabled children. It started when I met a disabled child as I was driving along Centre Street in Trenton, NJ. I noticed a child in a wheelchair being helped across the street by his father. I immediately pulled my car over to the side of the road, exited the car and ran across the street to catch up with the father. I opened my wallet and removed a handful of money. I handed him the

Lemon Juice

money because I felt he was in need, having a disabled child. I knew I had done the right thing and I continued doing 'the right thing,' for children and adults in need.

Handing out the money was a very easy thing to do however, on my way to work I felt that I was not doing enough unless I could help more people. The following day I stopped by Lenny's house. He was the child in the wheelchair. His grandmother, Mary, was taking care of him along with the grandfather, who I had thought was Lenny's father at that time. I spent about a half-hour with Mary to see what else I could do in addition to just giving them money. She showed me her bills and the assistance money that she was receiving from the government due to being impoverished and for taking care of Lenny. Each month they would be short $125.00. I told her do not worry, that I would send her $150.00 a month and that I would be there to help in the event of emergencies. It turned out that Lenny attended Mercer Day Training Center which focused on seriously disabled children. I got in touch with the person heading the organization and arranged to have a party at my horse farm for all the children in their charge. We had several parties at our farm but one stands out the most. It was at Christmas time.

The weather was in the 40s and sunny. I called my friend Larry and informed him what I was planning to do and needed his help to be Santa Claus. I was hoping for a white Christmas so that I could use one of my sleighs from my museum and a pair of horses or my farm tractor to drive Santa Claus around the farm, loaded with gifts for all the children. As the day approached for our event, the weather predicted was warm so regrettably there would be no sleigh ride with Santa Claus.

I was trying to figure out what we could do to excite the kids. The children were to arrive in several vans about 10:30am, at our property. All kinds of thoughts bounced through my head when one thing changed. It literally started to snow! Despite the weather prediction and high temperatures, it still snowed enough to put white highlights on the green pastures. We were a 'go.'

I had all the children and their attendants stationed in a former chicken coop, now converted to apartments. I drove the tractor and Larry was the Santa Claus in his outfit with gifts covering him and the sleigh in every direction. All the kids peered out of the glass pane windows that were fogged from the children's panting.

Every one of these kids were so excited and jumping up-and-down from happiness that this 90 foot building that was over 100 years old was literally vibrating throughout.

As Santa handed the gifts to each child, the excitement grew. Then I saw something that I was never accustomed to seeing in my life. If one child had a large gift (all unopened) and another child had a small one with no one knowing what the package contained, they would graciously offer the other child their gift. These kids of various religions and races loved each other. That night I was up with Marlene pumped with adrenaline and neither of us could sleep being so happy and grateful. I wrote a poem that these were God's children with

Lemon Juice

no knots in their stomach, trying to hide their feelings and emotions, so they were not tainted by society.

I felt being charitable was my purpose in life. I had done well in business and now it was time to give back. I believed I had been put on this earth to help those less fortunate than myself and I live by the dictum to give back everyday of my life. My maxim is: "**We should ask ourselves daily: "What can I do to make someone's life better today?**"

Chapter Twelve

Jail (again and again)

Back in the fifties and sixties, most cars were produced with standard black tires as a carryover from the prewar days when getting the material for whitewalls was relatively expensive. No dealer who traded an automobile with black tires would go to the expense of throwing out useable, but worn tires simply to replace them with a set of whitewalls, even though whitewall tires made the car look much more attractive and appealing to a potential buyer.

Certainly, if an automobile had very low tread - or none at all - there was the expense of getting new tires. Also, people purchasing automobiles wanted to purchase a vehicle with low mileage, believing that the car would have a longer lifespan in the care of the new owner.

Alleviating the extra expense of buying new tires, was an automotive service station nearby that could create deeper treads on a tire, making it much more appealing for a prospective buyer. They could also turn back the odometer, whether it be a wholesale transaction or to the retail public.

Lemon Juice

Don't get me wrong. They did not do anything illegal, because in those days there were no laws governing these practices.

The cars did not miraculously go through a life altering experience that turned them back to childhood. Plain and simple, dealers went to wherever they could have port-a-walls installed, which made a tire look like an actual bright whitewall tire, but wasn't.

To enhance the tread a couple of brothers that were proficient in re-grooving tires, used an electric hot iron that had a "V" shaped groove element at the end to create additional depth, which gave the appearance of a thicker tread. What it actually did was remove the precious little remaining rubber for the sake of getting a quick sale and maximizing profits. Also, on the premises was one person that would use tools sometimes called 'pics' to reach behind the odometer and rollback the miles to whatever the dealer wanted.

While selling cars from my house I would sometimes take one of my cars to get it serviced where car dealers would converge to have their cars 'enhanced.' What may have seemed even more surprising or even shocking, is that the dealers who had their tires re-grooved, would not have given a second thought to driving the cars themselves, even though they would not be as safe as they were prior to the treads being miraculously deepened.

Some dealers used to love having their mileage reset to 35,000 miles or 45,000 miles. However, every dealer stayed away from having the mileage turned back so that it would still

Jail (again and again)

appear to be above 50,000 miles, even if there were 99,000 actual miles on the car. Fifty thousand miles was no man's land. That was a no-no. It had to stay below 50,000 miles to make the car appealing.

Please don't think this was only practiced by used car dealers. Many times I would go to purchase cars from new car agencies and in their shop I saw electric power drills with the cable and a fitting that would attach to the back of a speedometer. The process would take several hours as it was a very slow, tedious procedure. They had someone watch it occasionally to make sure they didn't rollback the miles too far. They usually did this because they wanted to keep rolling back the odometer an in-house 'secret.' It wasn't a secret to any other dealer - just to the public. This practice was ongoing from the time the first automobile was produced and contained an odometer.

In the 1960s many car dealers that were wholesalers would bring their vehicles to our car lot at Northeast Autorama. Many times they brought me very attractive automobiles that ran very well and were good quality. There were very few - if any - dealers that did not roll back the mileage and nobody ever thought much of it.

One day, Arthur, a wholesaler, drove by my place with a gorgeous Oldsmobile two door hardtop with 88,000 miles. It was kept like new. It needed nothing, but I would not buy that car because the mileage was too high. That was on Monday. Two days later I found myself at the auction in Bordentown and there was Arthur's car now showing 32,000 miles. It brought several hundred dollars more than he had offered the car

Lemon Juice

to me. That upset me. It was the first time I realized how a customer must feel if they found out the mileage on their car had been turned back.

This realization prompted me to have a rubber stamp made that stated "I, the seller, hereby certify that the mileage appearing on_____ vehicle is true and accurate." There was a space for the dealer to sign. Every week when I went to the auction I would place the stamp's imprint on the back of my check and made sure the dealer signed it. I did not mind paying more for lower mileage cars. This lasted about a year until the auction insisted that I stop requiring this affirmation of mileage, fearing that they might be brought into a lawsuit as being part of a claim. I had nowhere to go without the auction for the volume of cars that we were selling.

I researched legislation that could possibly deal with turning back the mileage on automobiles and found nothing on the books whatsoever at that time which dealt with regulating odometer tampering.

My first call was to the District Attorney's office in Philadelphia, since I had sold an Assistant District Attorney an automobile. He told me he knew of nothing that addressed this issue and suggested that I get in touch with a State Representative or possibly even a State Senator. I then telephoned our State Senator and discussed with him at length the idea of introducing a bill or law into the Pennsylvania State Legislature, prohibiting the resetting of mileage.

Jail (again and again)

Sometime in 1972, odometer tampering became a law in the State of Pennsylvania and in the same year, it became a Federal law: The Federal Odometer Act of 1972, prohibiting the tampering of motor vehicle's odometers. I felt I was instrumental in protecting the public from these unethical practices, which had been perpetrated on the general public for decades.

Additionally, prior to the days of "Truth in Lending" also known as 'Regulation Z,' it was not uncommon for an automobile dealer to give the customer the price of the car and then quote whatever monthly payment the customer wanted to hear. Many unscrupulous dealers would go through the act of writing the payments in pencil simply to erase them when a customer left. Others would give the customer the exact payment then change the period of time for repayment. "Yes, your payments are $78.15 for only 24 months," when in fact the dealer knew that he was quoting it for 36 months.

We were seriously looking to build a long lasting business expecting to get as many repeat customers and referrals as possible. Many of the property houses knew what was happening and they did not care. They simply turned a blind eye knowing that they would place a mortgage against the customers' home. They were called 'prop' houses because they would only make loans to people who owned their homes or had equity in them. They in fact made the mortgage against each home but never told the customer. They were so greedy that they got into the act of packing a deal or loading it with unusual charges. If they had a customer who was easy, they

Lemon Juice

simply raised the payment amount by a few dollars per month and told them that included an 'auto club' fee.

A former governor in the State of Pennsylvania actually had interest to see that property houses sold "A and H Insurance." That was accident and health which was added to their monthly mortgage payments. It was an incredible rip-off. There was no 'auto club,' it simply gave the finance prop house more revenue. They made a fortune. I looked at many deals that we were happy to get financed because we had a large profit going for us, only to see the finance company making double the amount that we did.

There were charges for auto club, accident insurance, health insurance, plus they charged for prothonotary [*chief clerk*] fees and anything else that they could get away with. This was not done only to those people who were naïve, but to many intelligent people who possibly had a slow payoff loan somewhere so were unable to arrange a bank loan. These practices were sanctioned as being legal but were the closest thing to loansharking as could be.

While we would do anything to press a customer into delivery we would never quote a wrong payment nor would we give them the incorrect period of repayment. We did not fill out all of the finance contracts because it simply took too long and in most cases the forms were extremely burdensome and complicated. We would fill out the place on the contract that was totally noticeable, along with the correct down payment, the monthly installment and the period of repayment. Other dealers would not even do that much.

Jail (again and again)

During the late 60s there was a crusade in Congress to straighten out this abusive practice. Crackdowns were ordered. The practice filtered down through the states to the cities.

I was sipping coffee at my office at Northeast Autorama when I was informed that there was a warrant for my arrest as president of Estate Liquidators, Inc. I had no idea what was going on. I didn't do anything wrong. Why did they want to arrest me? Seems there were many reasons. The pressure was on the cities to set an example for other dealers and since we were advertising on television many times a week, we were one of their targets.

Since the inception of the Estate Liquidators, the district attorney had enmity for me at the obvious implication of the name. To keep the company legal, I always ran the following advertisements in the classified section of the newspapers. *"Wanted. Only the finest automobiles from Estates. Top dollar paid. Appraisals given. Call the Estate Liquidators."* By posting this advertisement I could always make a case that we were actively seeking to purchase the finest cars from estates. Occasionally we did. I could not help it if we only purchased one or two a year. This ad pissed off the District Attorney's Office, which was headed by Arlen Specter. His aides were out to get us. Their office had received complaints about the Estate Liquidators but there was nothing to them. People who had their cars financed through property houses tried to get out of their deals. This was impossible.

Customers were being prompted by the DA to state that they did not know the monthly payments nor the term of the

Lemon Juice

repayment, but this was a lie. It didn't do me any good knowing it because I was booked and fingerprinted. Me, Gene Epstein, a nice Jewish kid from Logan, sitting in jail with criminals - but then - I had spent time in jail once before, although, only briefly. Still, it was no fun being in jail no matter how short the duration.

I was placed in the first row of cells near the booking room. Looking around the cell, I vowed that whatever I did that got me here would never happen again. I was furious that my partners ran the business in such a way that they were unable to handle the complaints and stop anything from getting out of hand.

I called the guard at the front desk and told him I had to make a phone call. They looked at me as though I was a well respected citizen and treated me accordingly. They let me use the phone and I called for hoagies to be sent to the prison. I ordered enough for all of the guards at the front desk. When I get nervous I get hungry. No word from either of my partners until a couple of the longest hours had passed. Then Bobby come down to the Roundhouse Police Headquarters with Bob Simone. He was trying to reach a judge but it was getting late.

I sat in jail for hours waiting for a lawyer to get me out. I was arraigned in night court in the Roundhouse situated in Center City Philadelphia. The witnesses all claimed they signed loan papers that were blank. This was bullshit. But the judge saw this as being fit for a trial.

Jail (again and again)

My lawyer was a young, kind of aggressive and politically oriented person, Robert F. Simone. He lived across the street from my wife on the 5100 block of 11th Street in the Logan section of Philly. I knew him well. He had spoken with the district attorney who said they knew they did not have a case against us because the customers had written in their own handwriting that they knew the amount financed along with the payments and the length of the repayment. However, they claimed we never gave them a copy of the contract (which we denied), nor did we fill out other information.

The DA knew that we might not be the target that they were seeking, so they struck a deal. We agreed with Assistant District Attorney Swanson, to sign the consent decree, but never admit any guilt and agreeing that in the future all papers would be filled out prior to being signed. We did this. He also wanted the statement to be even more complete than simply relating to the financing, which went into any promises made by a salesman. We also agreed. The statement which he designed covered several areas which were not law but he wanted it that way. We were all glad that this case would not go to trial and thus we agreed.

I sarcastically said then I would go one step further. I would have the customers tape record statements that the papers they had were completely filled out. In reality, that's exactly what I did. It protected me, it protected my company and it protected the customer.

Virginia Knauer became President Nixon's Director of the new "Department of Consumer Affairs." The department which she headed was in the news constantly. Her son Wilhelm (Billy) Knauer was an assistant district attorney in Philadelphia and a customer of ours. He knew that most of the DA's case was bullshit. I told him that I wanted to have all the dealers use a disclosure statement similar to the one which we agreed to use under the consent decree. So off to the Washington I went.

I met with Frank McGlaughlin, one of the attorneys for the department. I stressed my feelings to have something like this pressed into some form of legislation. I wanted a level playing field for all dealers and their customers. Very shortly after that "Truth in Lending" became the law of the land and anytime a consumer's home was used as collateral for a purchase, they would have 72 hours to rescind the transaction.

They placed a small article in the Philadelphia Inquirer stating *"Auto Dealer Signs Consent Decree."* I did not like the negative press but it was certainly better than *"President of Northeast Autorama Sits In Jail,"* which I had envisioned.

Over the next year we had so much paperwork being signed along with tape recordings that we needed additional office space. I was determined not to have anymore negative press so I decided to turn around peoples' opinion. I wrote to different newspapers telling them about our success with our disclosure statement, which we used in our day-to-day business. I apprised them that I had conferred with the district attorney trying to cover all points of a transaction that might be vague.

Jail (again and again)

Between all the newspapers that I had written to with copies of our disclosure statements that were also sent to the Better Business Bureau, I received my first positive article in the Chamber of Commerce "Fortnight" - their monthly publication. Right there on page one was a copy of our disclosure statement having the headline *"Used Cars Without Catches."* They also copied our new guarantee which I instituted giving *"Free Lifetime Service"* to customers with any car purchase. I made copies of this and sent them once again to the media.

There was yet another thorn in the side of all new and used car dealers in the Philadelphia area and this thorn's name was Abe. Every dealer tried to stay far away from Abe and his new consumer group.

Abe would determine where to picket a business and at the drop of a hat would show up with his band of emissaries of disruption. It didn't matter how little the problem was or whom they were picketing, they were there to harass the car dealers. That little wiry guy sure knew how to get under a person's skin.

Weekly, Abe and his group picketed any place imaginable. Now, it was our turn. Abe was there in force demanding that we let a customer out of a deal and give him his money back because he said the car was a lemon. I told Abe that we did not build the car; we only sold them. He stated that he would continue picketing us unless we did as he demanded. To me, that was extortion! I told him to go fuck himself - and moments later he and his delegates of disturbance were outside my property with bullhorns in hand picketing Northeast Autorama.

Lemon Juice

Customers coming into our car lot were yelled at by Abe and his cohorts of chaos. The customers still made their purchases, even so, it certainly had to hurt our business. It would be foolish to think it didn't. I turned on my outside paging system and started a verbal battle with Abe blaring retorts at him over the loudspeaker system.

After one hour Abe and his group left our premises, not because of our verbal battle. Noooo, he left because Abe was scheduled to picket another dealer's lot and had to get going so that he could ruin someone else's day.

As pissed off as I was at him, I sort of admired him in a way. He had a cause to fight for and he pursued it fervently. Frankly, it was a relief to see him depart - and I hoped it would be for good. I had enough workload on my plate that I didn't need him compounding my day with aggravation. But there WAS more aggravation.

Over fifty years later I can still see the medium green colored 1962 Jaguar XKE 2+2 fixed head coupe, as referred to by the British, or by those in the USA, as simply a two door hardtop.

We had taken it in trade and one evening I had decided to leave behind the current car that I was driving and take this high performance sports car to Center City where I was going to the "Schvitz." The "Schvitz" was actually the Camac Baths, where one could relax and get a steam bath and an oak leaf massage. 'Schvitz' is a Yiddish word that means "sweat," and you certainly did sweat being in an environment where the heat constantly exceeded 110°.

Jail (again and again)

I paid no attention to a few very handsome men, later realizing that most were gay. It didn't make any difference to me as long as it was laissez-faire. I preferred 'hands-off' unless that other person was the masseuse.

Later that evening I was heading back home from Center City and decided to take the newest route home which was the Schuylkill Expressway that had just opened within the past few days.

I remember seeing a minor dusting of fresh snowflakes and to me it appeared as if I was the only driver on the road that evening and I probably was. How wrong I was. Behind the wheel cruising at about 75 miles an hour with virtually no traffic visible in either direction, out of my right eye as I passed the Girard Avenue overpass, I thought I saw a police car with flashing lights standing still. Looking back, I actually did. A few minutes more and I would be at the exit for the Roosevelt Boulevard or Route 1, both being the same.

I must have been doing more than 75 miles an hour and when I went to the exit, I came to an abrupt halt. There was a roadblock. Police cars with flashing lights on the roof facing the direction that I was heading. 'What the hell is going on?' I asked myself. I thought there was some type of emergency or perhaps an accident never thinking that the roadblock was there to stop ME. Is this ever going to end? Those thoughts went through my mind. I know that I tend to push boundaries, not accepting anything traditional if I felt that I could either improve something or make a change. But why in the world would the police be stopping <u>me</u>? I decelerated from about

Lemon Juice

60 miles an hour to zero. Facing me with headlights on high beams and flashers above the highway patrol cars were police officers with rifles and shotguns. 'This just can't be,' I thought to myself as I went to get out of the Jaguar.

One officer approached with a shotgun just a few feet away from me and pointing it directly at me. There's not much to say only 'Can I help you?' As opposed to why are all you idiots standing there looking to shoot me? Within a couple seconds I was flipped around by one of the officers with my hands stretched out on the roof of my Jaguar and then handcuffed. At that point I didn't think I'd be driving the Jaguar anywhere unless I was able to get behind the wheel and go straight home. I was certainly not going to argue with a bunch of State troopers that had shotguns pointed in my face.

One officer took the keys to my Jaguar as I was being pushed into the back of a patrol car and 15 minutes later the patrol car pulled up to the 'Roundhouse,' the Center City police prison or holding tank where I had briefly spent some time before. I was not feeling cocky, but was really shook up. I could not believe what was transpiring. I knew that I did not do anything that would cause all this commotion, yet it **was** happening and it was happening to **me**.

My first concern was how do I reach my wife, Marlene, to tell her what was going on. I was being charged by the highway police officer for resisting arrest and trying to flee the scene. Flee what scene? Did I commit a crime? Did I rob a bank? Something was going on that I did not understand. I asked to make a phone call since from watching so many television

Jail (again and again)

detective programs I remembered the police always permitted one phone call to be made by the incarcerated person. My request was denied. I told them that I was a businessman that was somewhat respected and had done nothing wrong with the exception of going 5 or 10 miles an hour over the speed limit. I certainly did not try to escape or outrace a police car. My explanation fell on deaf ears.

Thirty minutes later I was being escorted from the temporary cell to yet another police car and taken to Germantown and Haines where there was another police station. There, I was placed in a cell with a drunk who was out of it, after peeing on the wall in the cell. Looking back I can picture myself with a tin cup running up and back over the vertical steel bars trying to cause a commotion in order to get attention to find me a lawyer. Eventually I was permitted to make one phone call and I called Robert F. Simone, one of the top criminal lawyers in Philadelphia, who was a good friend of mine.

I told Robert what had happened and he told me I was being arraigned the next morning at 9 o'clock. He would get in touch with the judge on my behalf. He told me that he would have to give the judge one hundred dollars. I didn't give a damn as long as I could get out as soon as possible.

Waiting in the prison cell until the next morning, I was being escorted to the arraignment judge in handcuffs. The police officer gave his testimony and that alone was all that was needed since he stated that before he was on the highway patrol for Philadelphia, he was a Pennsylvania State trooper and he left out of frustration because a Jaguar was racing on

Lemon Juice

the turnpike and even though he had a high-speed Chrysler powered engine, he was unable to catch the Jaguar. He told the judge that he promised himself the next time he ever saw a Jaguar exceeding the speed limit he was going to arrest that person. 'That person' turned out to be **me**.

This highway patrol officer had some mental problems which the judge realized, however I felt comfortable knowing that Bobby Simone was there to defend me.

I called my wife, Marlene, from the police station to tell her I was in jail (again) all night long and to this day I don't know if she believed me.

I could not wait to get home and get into my bed to get some shuteye without fear of being peed on by a drunk and serving a long stretch in prison.

Alright, alright, alright, this was the third time I spent a brief time in jail, but this detention wasn't my fault. It was pure happenstance. I plead the Fifth…

Jail (again and again)

JAMES C. GREENWOOD
8th District, Pennsylvania

COMMITTEE ON COMMERCE
SUBCOMMITTEES:
HEALTH AND ENVIRONMENT
FINANCE AND HAZARDOUS MATERIALS
OVERSIGHT AND INVESTIGATIONS

COMMITTEE ON
EDUCATION AND THE WORKFORCE
SUBCOMMITTEES:
EARLY CHILDHOOD, YOUTH AND FAMILIES
POSTSECONDARY EDUCATION, TRAINING
AND LIFE-LONG LEARNING

Congress of the United States
House of Representatives
Washington, DC 20515-3808

2436 Rayburn Building
Washington, DC 20515
(202) 225-4276

District Offices:
69 E. Oakland Ave.
Doylestown, PA 18901
(215) 348-7511

1 Oxford Valley
Suite 800
Langhorne, PA 19047
(215) 752-7211

January 26, 1999

Mr. Eugene Epstein
Penn Oak

Dear Gene:

Thank you for your recent note on Project Donor. I appreciate the work you have been doing in this important area.

I am writing to inform you that I have again submitted a letter to Subcommittee Chairman Bilirakis to request a hearing on the critical issue of organ sharing. I have enclosed the letter for your review.

I will continue, on your behalf, to raise the awareness of this issue and work to frame the debate on the critical need to promote organ sharing; and specifically, to solicit a commitment for a hearing from Subcommittee Chairman Bilirakis.

As I am sure you understand, as a member of the committee of jurisdiction over the Health and Human Services Department, it is improper for me to endorse Project Donor before a review of the ethical issues.

In the meantime and as I indicated last year, I stand ready to call a meeting with HHS staff on your behalf to discuss organ sharing issues and Project Donor in more detail.

Sincerely,

James C. Greenwood

JCG: mg

Courtesy of The Honorable Congressman, James C. Greenwood

Lemon Juice

Richard M. DeVos

April 20, 2001

Mr. Eugene Epstein

Dear Mr. Epstein:

In honor of *National Organ and Tissue Donor Awareness Week* I wanted to take the opportunity to thank you for drafting the Senate proposal for organ donation. Your dedicated support of organ donation is truly remarkable. As a heart transplant survivor, I am a grateful beneficiary of determined efforts like yours that encourage others to be organ and tissue donors.

By setting such a marvelous example, you give hope to others. I salute you for that, as I share a similar mission in life – to be an encourager – a life enricher – and someone who motivates people to always have hope.

I've enclosed two copies of my latest book, *Hope From My Heart: Ten Lessons for Life*, which tells my personal story. I trust in some small way you'll find enjoyment and blessings in reading it.

Best wishes for continued success in all you do.

Sincerely,

Rich DeVos
Owner & Chairman, NBA Orlando Magic
Co-founder, Alticor

Courtesy of Richard M. DeVos

Jail (again and again)

THE IACOCCA FOUNDATION

April 11, 2008

Mr. Eugene "Gene" Epstein

RE: Presentation at Amelia Island Concours d'Elegance - 2008

Dear Gene:

Congratulations! As the winner of The Lee Iacocca Award you have been selected by your peers because you are not only outstanding in the car collector hobby but have been a constant supporter, both financially and emotionally, to a number of shows where the goal is to raise funds for various charities. This as you may know is a subject very close to me, since I've been trying to find a cure for diabetes for 25 years now. Everyday we are closer and I still carry the hope to find a cure in my lifetime.

The Award is presented to the person who has shown excellence in dedication to the preservation of an American automotive tradition. My award has been established to recognize you and all that you have done. I am honored to know you have chosen to further your hobby through exemplary actions and that the history of our automotive tradition is safe in your hands.

Please accept this Award in the spirit in which it is given. You are truly one of a few and well deserve The Lee Iacocca Award. I was especially struck about your program called "Common Ground Mission". I too, bring young people together each year at Lehigh University to participate at The Iacocca Institute and Global Village program. The only way our world is going to survive is if we all learn to respect our differences and embrace what we do have in common.

Sincerely,

Lee Iacocca

LI/ns

11150 Santa Monica Boulevard • Suite 400 • Los Angeles, CA 90025 • Tel 310.806.4013 • Fax 310.806.4062
17 Arlington Street • Boston MA 02116 • Tel 617.267.7747 • Fax 617.267.8544

Courtesy of The Iacocca Foundation

Lemon Juice

Free turkeys fill needy with joy

By Patricia Wandling
Courier Times

They came to Temple Shalom yesterday — widows, single parents, the disabled — for the second round of the turkey giveaway, sponsored by the Epstein family of Wrightstown.

While the pre-Thanksgiving giveaway was busier than yesterday's, there was a steady stream of people through the morning at the synagogue on Edgely Avenue in Bristol Township.

A total of 250 turkey vouchers and $5 "trimmings" vouchers were given away.

Among those who visited the synagogue were two Falls women who said they're trying to support their families on meager incomes.

"This is wonderful," said Rita E. Ryan, who has three sons. "A lot of people working a $5-an-hour job can't make it."

Her friend, Donna McCrory, echoed Ryan's remarks. "I have one child, and I appreciate all the help I can get. It's hard to buy a turkey when you're low income."

"This is very nice. It's good for the community to know you can get help," said a silver-haired widow from Bristol Township.

And another woman, due to have her first child this week, said she has been out of work because of medical complications with her pregnancy and struggles to pay her bills.

"This is helping a lot of people. It's going to help me," she said. "It's a nice thing to do, and I appreciate it."

By 11 a.m. more than 100 of the 250 turkey vouchers had been given away. Then Gene Epstein, who organized both turkey giveaways, took the rest to the state public assistance office in Bristol Township where he planned to give them to those applying for assistance.

The vouchers for turkey and trimmings are good for one month, said Epstein.

In November, more than 300 turkeys and $5 vouchers were handed out to needy families.

Yesterday's turkeys were donated by the Gene and Marlene Epstein Family Humanitarian Fund, Prime Bank, Alderfer's Antique Auction, the board of the Delaware Valley Philharmonic Orchestra and supporters of Jim Greenwood.

Courtesy of the Courier Times

Jail (again and again)

Dara Gever, a Jewish teen who's an 11th-grader at Council Rock High South; Joanna Raines, a Christian teen who's a 10th-grader at Council Rock North; and Muzammil Hasan, a Muslim teen who's a 10th-grader at Council Rock North are among a group of students who will travel to Israel as ambassadors of tolerance. PHOTOS BY JAY CRAWFORD / COURIER TIMES

A journey of faith

Muslim, Christian and Jewish teens will travel to Israel to learn about the culture and each other's faith.

By ELIZABETH FISHER
COURIER TIMES

Wrightstown philanthropist Gene Epstein's dream to foster understanding among religious groups will become reality Dec. 26, when 45 high school students — Jews, Muslims and Christians — leave for a 10-day trip to Israel, a country that is the bedrock for all three faiths.

It was nearly a year ago when Epstein, never known to think small, decided the best way to tackle the sectarian violence that severs communities and neighbors around the world is to start with the young. That's how the Common Ground Mission was born — and that's the banner under which Epstein hopes it will fly every year.

The best part is that the students don't have to pay for the trip, which averages about $2,000 for each traveler. The group will spend 10 days meeting with young people, visit youth groups and spread their

Council Rock North teacher Dave Greenockle (center) will help chaperone Dara, Joanna and Muzammil on the trip. "Our purpose is to draw upon similarities, not to resolve the Middle East crisis," said Greenockle.

To help

Donations can be sent to the Jewish National Fund, c/o Common Ground Mission, 2100 Arch St., Third Floor, Philadelphia, PA 19103.

well guarded at all times.

Muzammil said he looks forward to meeting Israeli and Palestinian peers.

"It's our world and we have to live together. I want to see our group bonding and getting along," said Dara Gever, a Jewish teen who's an 11th-grader at Council Rock High School-South in Northampton.

Dara admits to being a little nervous about going to the embattled territory, but she said she believes it's more important to go than to ignore the opportunity. "You cannot give into fear," she said.

Muzammil Hasan, a 10th-grader at Council Rock High School-North in Newtown Township, said his mother initially had reservations but was persuaded that security would be tight and the kids will be

Courtesy of the Courier Times

Lemon Juice

Courtesy of the Courier Times

Jail (again and again)

WRIGHTSTOWN

Couple wants to aid veterans who need help

By GEORGE MATTAR
STAFF WRITER

The economy is tough for many today. Imagine what it's like for a war veteran who comes home from Iraq or Afghanistan and cannot find a job, or is facing a rough time.

Local humanitarians and philanthropists Gene and Marlene Epstein of Wrightstown want to help.

"We need to know how many wounded Iraq and Afghanistan veterans from Bucks County are in dire financial straits so that we can determine how much money needs to be raised or those families of service people that have been killed that need help also," Gene Epstein said. "They will need to prove financial need and give us permission to verify their need."

Epstein is known for helping the less fortunate.

He said he will donate $25,000 to a matching fund to help the vets, if the public would donate the other $25,000.

First, Epstein said he must find and identify needy veterans or needy families of military members who died. This offer applies to Bucks County veterans only.

"I want this to be a community project. I have had great success in seeing the community help itself and, although I never served in a war, I want to help our soldiers who helped protect our freedom and now may need our help," he said.

The Epsteins have called their latest venture Helping Our Veterans.

"It will be a matching fund. Hopefully we can get more. My wife and I recently did a matching donation drive for the Bucks County Food Bank. I told them I'd give them $15,000. They raised $38,000."

"This type of response inspires me and my wife to continue giving. It gives us an incredibly good feeling. We find out about those in need through this newspaper. Those are the kind of stories you don't find or see anywhere else. Without the Courier Times, we would not know of all the misfortune out there," he said. "These are the kind of stories you don't see on the Internet or on television."

Epstein said he got the idea to help needy vets while walking outside the Richboro Shopping Center close to Memorial Day.

"Someone was selling poppies. I told her to give me her address and I would send her a check late in the week. I got to thinking about our servicemen and women. I was crying inside because I am grateful for all they do for us," he said. "Every day they put their lives on the line and we sit home complaining about the price of gasoline. My concern is our government is not providing enough support for them."

If anyone knows of a veteran or his family in need, send all correspondence to the Gene and Marlene Humanitarian Fund, P.O. Box 28, Penns Park, PA 18943.

George Mattar can be reached at 215-949-4165 or gmattar@phillyBurbs.c

Courtesy of the Courier Times

Lemon Juice

Thursday, August 25, 1994 3C

■ COUNCIL ROCK/EDUCATION

Resident: Use closed school for day care

Wrightstown resident Gene Epstein has a grand vision for the old Richboro Elementary School, a low-cost, not-for-profit day care center for children and the elderly.

By Chris English
Courier Times

While the district reportedly considers an offer from Northampton Township to buy the old Richboro Elementary School, resident Gene Epstein is pushing for another deal.

Epstein, of Wrightstown, has sent a letter to Superintendent Dave Blatt urging the school board to reject Northampton's offer and turn the old school into a low-cost, not-for-profit day care center for children and the elderly.

"I have been informed that Northampton Township is trying to acquire the property," the letter reads. "I implore you and the board members not to let this happen.

"There is an opportunity to serve the community in a way not conceived of before that will benefit the perception of the entire board by reaching out beyond the education of our children to help parents and their parents."

Blatt said he has spoken to Epstein, has read the letter, and will mail it to all nine school board members for their consideration.

"In all my discussions with Mr. Epstein, his focus has been on the needs of the community, and a desire to better our overall community," Blatt said. "The concept is a worthy one.

"Certainly, there are some considerations the legal minds should investigate. I would want to research, and I am sure the board would want to research, the legalities and liability associated with a school district coordinating these kinds of activities."

Under Epstein's proposal, the district would maintain ownership of the building. He thinks the day care center could be staffed mostly by volunteers — ments to the building for such a use would not be too costly.

"I've been through it and the building is pretty darn solid," said Epstein, who also has suggested some other uses, including a "mini-theater" or "performing arts center."

He has offered to oversee the facility for $1 a year, and thinks costs to users could be kept to a minimum.

Epstein, a commercial real estate investor, made an offer to buy the old school about two years ago. It was rejected by the district.

"I could make a fortune with the place, but I don't need any more income," he said. "I want to see that people in the community are served. The school board, for basically no extra dollars, can perform an incredible service.

"In two to five years, if the whole thing turns out to be borderline, they can always sell it and it will only be worth more. I can't conceive of this not being a winner."

While sources have told the Courier Times that attorneys for Northampton and Council Rock are negotiating a sale, Northampton supervisor Pete Palestina, would only say an offer to buy the school made over a year ago, has been "resurrected" and is, "still on the table."

The offer, according to Palestina, is a "$360,000 straight cash deal" for both the old school and a 7-acre plot of vacant land owned by the district on Township Road. He said plans for the two sites are not formalized, but the old school could become some kind of recreational facility and the Township Road site a new substation for the Tri-Hampton Rescue Squad.

The old Richboro school, on Route 232 near the intersection with Route 332, has been vacant since 1989, with several poten-

Courtesy of the Courier Times

Jail (again and again)

■ GIVE-A-CHRISTMAS

Epstein Family Humanitarian Fund sends a challenge

Just in...

■ "We at the Epstein Family Humanitarian Fund would like to match an individual (not business or corporate) donation of at least $500 ...with a total of all matching funds not exceeding $2,500. We wish to congratulate all those volunteers at the Give-A-Christmas Fund and the Bucks County Courier Times for their dedicated community service. Without the constant exposure of this fine program the fund would have little chance to reach its well deserved goals."

■ Loretta Warren from The Pines Tavern contributes $100 and hopes that all fellow Bucks County tavern owners will also give generously.

■ Jack and Brigitte Krauss include a gift of $100 to today's total to help some less fortunate families enjoy the beauty of the Christmas season.

How it works...

The Bucks County Courier Times and the Levittown-Bristol Kiwanis Club have co-

How to help...

Names and addresses of persons needing assistance may be mailed to Give-A-Christmas, P.O. Box 129, Levittown, PA 19058.

For a complete list of contributors,

Bucks County Courier Times
Wednesday, December 21, 1994

B

Courtesy of the Courier Times

Lemon Juice

Courtesy of the Courier Times

Courtesy of the Courier Times

Jail (again and again)

BUCKS COUNTY COMMUNITY COLLEGE
Scholarships enable students to realize dreams

Courtesy of the Courier Times

BUCKS COUNTY COMMUNITY COLLEGE
Fund bridges tuition gap for low-income families

Courtesy of the Courier Times

Lemon Juice

Snapshots

Dinner gift certificates

Thanks to the generosity of a Bucks County philanthropic family and a rabbi, a Lower Bucks synagogue will be presenting needy families in Lower Bucks with $2,500 in turkey dinner gift certificates during the holidays.

The sum is being donated by the Epstein Family Humanitarian Fund ($2,300) of Wrightstown and Rabbi Allan Tuffs ($200) of Congregation Temple Shalom of Levittown.

Gene Epstein

Those in need should stop by the synagogue, located at 2901 Edgely Road, between noon-4 p.m. today and 9 a.m.-4 p.m. tomorrow. Recipients must present identification showing they are on welfare or SSI. Each will receive a certificate redeemable at a local supermarket.

Rabbi Allan Tuffs

Gene, Marlene and children Ellen and Robert Epstein operate the Epstein Family Fund. The Epsteins have been doing community service for 30 years. Recently, they raised $5,000 to help build a homeless shelter for Sister Mary Scullion's mission in Philadelphia.

The Epsteins are not members of Temple Shalom, but enlisted the synagogue's involvement.

Courtesy of the Courier Times

Jail (again and again)

The Beit Guvrin Reservoir in Besor, Northern Negev, Israel, which Gene and Marlene had build and donated in Matilda "Bille" Epstein's name c. 2012, and inscribed as follows:

"THIS RESERVOIR WAS ESTABLISHED THANKS TO THE GENEROSITY OF MATILDA "BILLE" EPSTEIN AND GENE AND MARLENE EPSTEIN"

Courtesy of the Jewish National Fund

Lemon Juice

Courtesy of the Epstein Family Humanitarian Fund

Chapter Thirteen

Hammertoe

After a while this business will get to the best of people. Not that I was the best, but I was up there with the hardest workers. My backside was dragging going through the ritual of heading to Bordentown, New Jersey every Wednesday, getting the automobiles detailed, running ads in the newspapers, selling the vehicles and having to deal with the occasional irate customer. Then heading to Manheim, Pennsylvania for another automobile auction on Fridays. I left work late each evening and I arrived first thing every morning. This routine was sucking the energy out of me. I needed a vacation but I was reluctant to take a break, feeling guilt over leaving my partner Bobby to handle the entire operation by himself. During that time my hammertoe was killing me.

I have always had problems with my feet since I was able to stand on them. As a child I remember the school nurses taking a blue ink impression for a footprint in elementary school to see if I was in need for corrective footwear. The physical therapist wanted to repeat the ink test because there was just

Lemon Juice

one big blue smear which showed no definition. It obviously required attention.

Later, I had a constant ingrown toenail in my large toe which never healed. I was a victim of an unscrupulous foot doctor who managed to clean the pus from the toenail, which accumulated daily, and then pretend to trim out the ingrown part of the nail bed, only to have the same problem recur the following day. This then became my schedule for nearly three months when I was about 14 years old.

I attended Central High School, which was near the Jewish Hospital. On my way home from a bowling alley my foot was throbbing. I felt there was only one way of getting relief, so I stopped into the hospital. Before long I was being held down by two nurses and a doctor while an intern was flushing out the poisons from my toe. He actually placed a large syringe into my toe and left the needle there while he kept changing the syringes that filled with pus. I screamed in pain as any normal human being would have. I thought I saw my young life flash before my eyes!

As I screamed in pain, one of the nurses poured orange juice into my mouth so that I would gag and stop screaming. Finally, they wrapped my toe, cut a hole in my shoe and sent me home. Boy, if I knew then what I know now about malpractice I would have probably owned the hospital.

Upon reaching my 15th birthday, I was once again beset by agony. I simply peddled my bicycle down the street looking for a foot doctor. At this time we lived in a new neighborhood

Hammertoe

where my mother and I opened up a candy store. I saw a sign which stated 'Podiatrist, Chiropodist.' I got off my bike and stepped inside his office. There, I met this really super doctor. He looked at my black and blue toe and called a surgeon for advice. He immediately called my mother. It was the first time that someone wanted to speak to my mother about my toe. He said it was urgent that I have an immediate operation. The next day I was being operated on by Dr. Newman. He was supposedly the first chiropodist permitted to perform foot surgery.

I loved both of those doctors because they gave me relief. Dr. Newman found a hook piece of my nail that was purposely left there so that the infection would constantly reoccur, making me dependent upon the prior foot doctor. The infection was so bad that I almost lost my foot. Needless to say, since that operation I have not had one ingrown toenail. I did however have a hammer toe adjoining that big toe which stuck up in the knuckle and constantly rubbed against the inside of my shoe. The pain was bearable even though sometimes it flared up and became extremely painful.

One day, it had flared up severely again. Probably because the day before was a very long day at the Bordentown auto auction which meant running from one car lane to another and then hopping in to test drive each car and handing in my reports prior to paying for the vehicles. Not that this day was different than any other day before, but it had been building up and I knew that it was time to have the hammertoe surgically corrected.

Lemon Juice

I had put it off for far too long and my handsome Bostonian dress shoes always looked funny since the shoe store would always have to stretch the area where my hammer toe was positioned. I decided it was time to permanently address this problem and a couple days later I was in the hospital.

The operation was set for 12 o'clock the day. The nurses administered all kinds of drugs to put me out. I did not fall asleep. I was definitely wide awake. The doctor was standing in the operating room as I was brought in on a gurney. They covered my lower body with a sheet and started to work. I told Dr. Newman to be careful. One of the nurses got hysterical. "Doctor Newman, the patient is still awake!!" The doctor told her that she didn't know what she was talking about and that I was just hallucinating. I told him that I felt a burr so to please sand the joint down on my toe very smoothly. Once again the nurse was visibly shaken by my comments realizing that I was fully awake. But again, the doctor dismissed her concern, insisting that "He's hallucinating." At that point I said "Fuck you! There's a burr there and I can feel it." He instructed the anesthesiologist to increase the units of anesthesia, for now he believed that I was truly awake.

After surgery, I was wheeled back to my hospital room and within two hours I was screaming in pain. The nurse had administered some painkillers. I looked across the semiprivate room and only saw the back of another patient. He had a broken back and did not complain. I did. Shit. The pain was killing me! More nurses and more painkillers and still no relief. It was a long evening and the nurses were fed up attending

Hammertoe

to me. I kept apologizing to the man in the next bed. He graciously said that he understood.

Now it was 10 o'clock at night and the nurses would no longer respond. I rang the buzzer repeatedly. No response. I turned lights on but could not get them. I finally resorted to calling for an outside telephone line for the main number. When the phone was answered at the hospital's front desk, I asked for the head nurse. She answered. The nurses were all playing cards down the hall. I could hear them through the phone when she answered. I told her that if she doesn't get her ass over here right now and get something to relieve the pain, that I would hit her in the face with a chair.

Moments later she came in and started to look at my arms. I thought she was going to give me a needle. Instead, she asked if I were a drug addict. At that point I wanted to kill her. She called the doctor at home and was given permission to administer heavy painkillers. I still could not sleep and the excruciating pain continued unabated. No way was I going to stay in that hospital for three more days.

I called Sam, my chauffeur, at 6 o'clock in the morning and told him to pick me up. The nurses were yelling at me. The head nurse told me that she would not discharge me. I told Sam, my Scottish chauffeur, to pick up a chair and hit the first person that would not let me out of the hospital. Everyone backed off. At 7:30am I was in my bed at home. I felt better but the toe was still throbbing. I had a full bottle of Demerol, which the doctor had ordered for me, but I chose not to take it since I had already been given so much pain medicine. I laid there

Lemon Juice

quietly in bed thinking of the past few days and why I decided to go to the hospital. After admitting to myself that it was a way to get a few days vacation without feeling guilty, the pain subsided - albeit temporarily.

A few days later the toe was still swollen and there was a significant amount of pain. Dr. Newman told me to come over to his office and Jack Gordon, Bobby's father, drove me there. Dr. Newman wanted to give me a series of five Cortisone shots to reduce the swelling. He had a vial of Cortisone and a syringe, which he injected into the swollen toe at its farthest point. I screamed from pain never feeling anything like this in my life. Jack Gordon held his chest - he felt faint and almost had a heart attack when he saw me rise out of the chair. I refused to have another injection and told Dr. Newman that the next surgery would be to remove my toe because I wasn't going to put up with this pain much longer.

The following week Bart Goldsmith, my sales manager at Northeast Autorama, suggested that I go see Dr. Vincent de Stefano, who was the orthopedic surgeon for the Philadelphia Eagles. Bart got me an appointment much quicker than I could have gotten one for myself and before I knew it, I was having x-rays taken in Dr. de Stefano's office. He looked at the x-rays and said that Dr. Newman did everything correctly, however there was a small burr that even with magnifying glasses Dr. Newman would be unable to detect. Over the next 50 years whenever the weather gets rainy and chilly, that toe reminds me of these incidents.

Chapter Fourteen

Dressed to Kill

In preparation for graduation at Olney High School, expecting to graduate, all students were instructed by their homeroom counselor to dress up for their individual photos that would appear in the graduation year book. I was not a clotheshorse by any means and did not have a suit to wear for my graduation photograph so I had to borrow a suit jacket from my brother Mickey. I wore a white shirt with a collar that was too big and dungarees with the suit jacket since the photograph only showed the upper part of my body. That was when I was 17 years old.

It bothered me that I didn't have much in the way of nice clothes. By the time we opened up Broad Street Auto Center, I had purchased a couple of suits.

Having liverwurst and mayonnaise on a bagel several mornings a week at the luncheonette close to my car lot and always picking up one or two Tastykake lemon pies to wash it down, my 163 pound high school physique was getting unrecognizable. Our evening meals were usually an enormous

Lemon Juice

corned beef sandwich from Kincus's Restaurant on Broad Street.

I was purchasing slacks at SID'S haberdashery on Broad Street, about one mile south of our business, when the owner told me that I would have to go from a size 36 waist, that I was wearing, to a size 38. At graduation my waist was 32 inches. I told Sid that he just lost a customer until I lost some weight.

Bobby had an idea, since he also wanted to lose weigh, we both bought memberships to Roger Serven Health Club in Jenkintown. We pledged to each other that we would keep pushing on until we lost the desired weight. After the second visit we both wanted to know what the cancellation penalty was. I forget the amount but we negotiated something and never went back. We did however start to diet and I wrote down everything I ate while looking up the calories in a small palm size book.

Six months later, I was down to a size 34 inch waist. Having our new facility on Roosevelt Boulevard with a higher quality of automobiles and a significantly more astute customer, I decided that I would have a suit custom made. Ironically the owner of the men's custom clothier was also named Sid. But these two Sids had no DNA in common. They couldn't be more different if they tried.

I went from the suit maker on Caster Avenue a short distance to a custom shirt maker on Bustleton Ave. After wearing my first custom made suit, I became more conscious of my reduced

Dressed to Kill

weight feeling that I was looking pretty good after peering into the mirror at myself, so I wanted to look even better.

A young and somewhat portly physician who had just started his practice in my neighborhood told me that since my allergies were so bad I should eliminate all dairy products and anything that contained wheat, rye or barley. I went from having a six egg omelet with a side order of bacon and a bowl of oatmeal to a cup of black coffee and one-half grapefruit for breakfast. There were no more hamburger sandwiches to eat for lunch so I began eating salads looking forward everyday to a large Cesar salad made without eggs or croutons. Without ever eating any bread, nor dairy products; each and every day only eating salads and more salads, many topped with grilled chicken or shrimp.

By the time I went back to Sid the suit maker, my waist was 32 inches. At the same time my energy levels were improving and my allergies were very controllable without the discomfort that bothered me all my life.

I had Sid alter my first suit and then ordered additional suits made of Turkish kid mohair. Back in the early 1960s custom made suits cost about $350 - today they would cost around $3,500. Everyday at work my employees and my customers always saw me dressed impeccably.

While my wife and I were on a short junket to Las Vegas, I purchased a gold owl's head ring that was loaded with diamonds. We went to see Don Rickels perform and had a front row table. I was wearing a plum colored Turkish kid

Lemon Juice

mohair suit with a lighter color coordinated shirt and a dark plum tie. Don Rickles, after embarrassing as many people in the audience as he possibly could, looked over to me and said "So, who's the Jew with a big nose wearing a purple suit?"

I remember my feet hurting since I was wearing a brand-new pair of black Bostonian shoes that looked great but they were killing me. I slid them off under the table until Rickles' act was over. When I went to put the shoes back on my feet, I could not get inside the shoes. Both feet were swollen. There I was, the handsome young man who entered showing off his custom clothes and leaving walking through the hotel, restaurant and casino sheepishly with my shoes in my hand.

As a hobby I was collecting horse drawn carriages and refinishing them at my house whenever I had time away from work. Two of my carriages had wicker bodies and a parasol that would cover the occupants to protect them from the sun. I needed to have new parasols made since the 100-year-old material on the carriages were falling apart. There was an Amish man doing work for me in Intercourse, PA. I asked him if he knew anyone who made parasols. He recommended Frankford and Sons on Frankford Avenue, which was only 2 miles from Northeast Autorama. I bought my first two parasols to get restored and was tickled pink to find out how beautiful their work was. In their office they had an original walking stick case with a curved glass lid displaying over two dozen walking sticks. I asked them the age of the case and was told that it was in the shop since they opened in the early 1900s.

Dressed to Kill

Upon returning to bring them another parasol to restore, I inquired about purchasing their walking stick case; $500 later I was loading it in sections into my car. A beautiful piece of furniture to add to my rustic recreation room, however it did not have any walking sticks in it. I then started to look at local antique auctions and could not be held back from purchasing walking sticks that I thought were unusual and attractive. The reason for digressing is that all these things come together.

I started to pose in front of the full length mirror in my dressing room at home and then picked up one of my walking sticks and felt that it completed the picture.

Within a year I had so many custom suits, sport jackets and custom made shirts, that I had to write a small post-it note to put on the inside of my closet door stating that for each suit I had a choice of three different shirts, ties and a choice of 20 different cufflinks. To complete the picture I also had a choice of several different walking sticks.

No one at any of the automobile auctions for decades ever remembered seeing me without being impeccably dressed and with an antique walking stick in hand.

Every week I would get a haircut at Armand and Dario's near Northeast Autorama. Dario would walk around after trimming my hair looking at me at different angles holding a mirror behind my head so I could see if anything was out of place. The manicurist in the meantime was taking care of my fingernails. After 15 minutes of leaving from my haircut, Dario would call without fail. "Is it still okay?" he would ask, almost sounding

Lemon Juice

fearful. I looked in the mirror and if I saw one hair out of place I would tell him "I'm coming right over." Every third or fourth time I would make a return trip.

The custom shirt maker on Bustleton Avenue in Northeast Philadelphia, had made 15 custom shirts for me. I would not wear them fresh from being made. Instead, I insisted they go to the Chinese laundry across the street from the shirt maker, as I did with all my other shirts.

At home on Saturday night after showering and starting to dress for a delicious meal at Blue Bell Inn, I put on one of the shirts. It fit well to my now very trim physique - however I noticed that there was a small crease in the collar. I took the shirt off and put on another shirt. The exact same crease occurred on that second collar as with all the rest of them. Turns out, the shirt maker never removed the collar stays when he had the Chinese laundry clean and press the shirts, so all the collar stays made an indentation in all the collars.

I was furious and started to rip off one collar after the other until I removed all 15 collars. I was ready to cancel going out to dinner that night because I thought it would be terrible to be seen with a crease in my collar. In another section of my closet, I found another shirt that would do for the evening.

Monday morning I was at Harris the shirt makers with all 15 shirts. "Do these over and make sure you don't fuck up again."

Quicker than I thought possible, I received a call from Harris on Wednesday that my shirts were ready and he was going to drop them off at my house. I asked him emphatically "Are they done correctly this time?" He assured me they were and delivered them to my house. At least I could be seen in public in the future without a crease in my collar, nor a hair out of place! OK, I admit it, people might think I'm a bit of a throwback to the Victorian era when men were gentlemen and dressed accordingly. But I like to think I simply take pride in my appearance.

One guy who didn't give a shit about his appearance was Big Moe Wasserman.

Years after Big Moe was extricated from a tiny MG roadster, he lost his business and was looking for a job. At the same time Northeast Autorama was advertising in the Philadelphia newspapers for another salesperson.

Big Moe applied for the sales position and was hired immediately because of his extensive experience in selling used cars. There was one drawback. Moe was a slob. A big fat slob. Moe spoke with a mumbled voice but everyone had to make sure they were standing at least 5 feet away if they were going to engage in a conversation with him, because as he gargled his words, saliva would spray out from his lips in every direction for several feet around, especially when he spoke forcefully. I think it was a defensive mechanism when he got nervous because he could speak to someone over the phone with clarity without spitting on the phone.

Lemon Juice

Moe weighed over 300 pounds and was about 5x5. You could see every meal that he had eaten in the past week just by looking at his tie.

I don't think he attained that bulbous weight eating ordinary meals. He was a grabber. If you were eating and he was nearby, one would have to protect their food or lose it.

About 2 to 3 miles south of Northeast Autorama was one of our favorite places for fresh hard-shell crabs and clams. Since it was so close we could be there in less than 10 minutes, squeeze in a lunch and head back to work.

One day Moe asked me to bring him back clams on the half-shell. "Don't get me those little baby pieces of shit. Get me nice sized ones," he spit out across the room.

I looked in the restaurant's display cases and saw a variety of clams. Some definitely were small while others were medium to large. "Chester - What do you have in the way of clams that are enormous?" I asked the owner. He told me everything that was edible was on display, however in the back he had chowder clams. I asked what they were and he brought out one to show me. Oh my god! I thought these things are enormous. "Give me a half a dozen of those, Chester," I instructed him. He asked me did I want a recipe for clam chowder since he expected these enormous clams to be diced up and put into a soup stock. "No thanks. I just want to get these for a pig." I walked out with six of the largest and heaviest clams I've ever seen in my life.

Dressed to Kill

Returning to Northeast Autorama with a container filled with clams on the half-shell, I placed them on my desk. I did not put the container on Moe's desk on purpose because I don't think he liked to eat food unless it belonged to someone else. "Moe, I just ate a half-dozen of these clams. They were so delicious I had to bring some back." And I walked out of the office pretending that I was going to just check out the inventory. Less than two minutes later I walked up to my desk and the insulated foam container holding the enormous clams was open and only two clams were left. They looked so big that I thought someone would need a crane to lift them up.

"You ate my clams you sonofabitch!" I said pretending to be upset when he responded that he thought I had bought them for him. "At this point you might as well finish them," which he did stuffing those huge clams into his mouth. Even today, I can't believe that anyone could consume those enormous chowder clams. Surprisingly, he never dropped parts of those clams onto his tie. The only indication of what he ate was red sauce on his blue tie. He never realized that we were laughing hysterically in one of our sales offices.

My daughter reminded me of another incident involving sloppy Big Moe.

Across the street from our car lot was a fast food hamburger place. Several times a week one of our salespeople would take our order across the boulevard and return, usually with a double cheeseburger and a side order French fries for anyone that wanted it.

Lemon Juice

One day, my sales manager came to work and showed me something he picked up at a novelty store. It was a realistic looking rubber hamburger. I guess at this point you realize what happened next. We ordered one of the double cheeseburgers that was smothered with Russian dressing and removed the bottom hamburger, replacing it with the rubber one. Everyone knew what I was doing with the exception of Moe who was finishing up with his customer. The bait was easily set by simply leaving the sandwich unattended on one of the salesmen's desks.

Quicker than the speed of light, the sandwich was unwrapped and in Big Moe's mouth. Somehow he bit into it, but not all the way. He tried again with no success and slid the hamburger out holding it in his right hand with Russian dressing dripping from it. He kept waving it up and back and said "This is the toughest hamburger I ever ate. I'm calling those bastards up!" Which he did. In my mind I thought why tell him now? Moe was yelling at the manager who apologized profusely and told Big Moe to please bring the sandwich back and they would give him a replacement, plus an extra sandwich for his trouble.

I never saw him move so fast. He grabbed the rubber hamburger, slid it back in between the slices of bread and put the wax paper wrapper back around it, jumped in the car and headed off to the hamburger joint.

The manager apologized to Moe in person and handed him two double cheeseburgers with Russian dressing. Just as Moe was leaving, the manager got his attention and called him back.

Dressed to Kill

"Hey! What are you trying to do?" The manager asked Big Moe. "This is a RUBBER hamburger!!" Moe said "That's what I've been telling you all along, it tastes like rubber," as he undulated out the door.

When he returned to work, we expected him to be pissed off at us, but that didn't happen.

"I'm never going back to that joint again. The sandwiches may taste good, but they're hard as rubber."

From the same ad for a salesman that attracted Big Moe, another salesman had also applied for the job, whose surname escapes me but I recall his given name was Andy. He was a Waspish fellow in appearance, who stood 6 feet tall with a stocky build and long gray hair.

He had automotive experience selling used cars and new cars at a well known dealership in the area. When Andy applied for a job, he asked for a demo car since he had been given one as a perk at his previous job. I told him that we do not give sales people a demo car, however if he needed transportation just to come from his home in Levittown to our car lot, which was about a 10 mile drive, I would supply him with the dealership's Jeep and give him $10 a week for expenses. This was the same Jeep that I used in numerous commercials on television with the well known disc jockey personality, Joe Niagara.

I told Andy that we had a sign to go on the roof of the Jeep that would say *"No money down at Northeast Autorama."* He agreed to use the Jeep with the signage as his "demo"

Lemon Juice

automobile and was receptive to the sales position. He had no idea what the sign would look like.

I placed a call to a sign company in the Frankford section of Philly. We designed a sign that was 4 feet high and 8 feet long, which was obviously too large to go onto the roof of this small Jeep. But I figured out how to get it fastened onto the roof, albeit, not designed for high speed driving

They made two signs: both sides were painted with a fluorescent 'Day-Glo' red background sporting yellow and black lettering, that would be visible from ether side. In fact, the colors were so eye popping, the sign would be visible from any of the six states bordering Pennsylvania.

I made a brace using two by fours for these enormous signs to rest on the roof. From the top of the signs I used galvanized chains to fasten the signs to the rain gutters and screwed them in place. We used a pair, one on the front side and one on the rear side. The sign was actually designed to sit in the gas station across the street from my car lot to attract potential customers, but I felt having the sign on the Jeep and being driven daily would be even better advertising.

While the sign was being constructed and painted, Andy had sold a couple cars and was very happy with himself. Then he saw his new transportation and was somewhat shocked.

"Are you guys crazy? You said a "sign" — this is a billboard!" He bellowed.

Dressed to Kill

"What's the big deal?" I asked. "A sign is a sign. You should carry your business cards with you to hand out to people whenever you stop." I thought that was far-fetched but you never know how you might get a customer and you should use every possible opportunity.

There was a drawback to this large sign, besides being embarrassing driving that Jeep with a hamburger painted on the panel of the body and a sign nearly as large as the vehicle, the drawback was the wind. Having such a large sign on the roof made the vehicle unstable. I took it out for a test drive and when I made a turn, I realized that the next time I would have to do it very, very slowly since there was a chance the vehicle could tip over as it rolled on only a couple wheels in the turn.

Andy had settled down and certainly selling a couple cars prior to driving his new 'demo' may have helped his attitude toward the Jeep.

At 9:00pm when we closed for business, Andy hopped into the Jeep and drove home. The 15 to 20 minute trip took Andy a little over an hour. It wasn't because people stopped and asked about buying a car. Nooooo, it was because once he reached 20 miles an hour he had almost no control over the car, since the 4x8 sign acted as an enormous sail. Andy could only drive the Jeep at 15 miles an hour and slower when making turns.

He had butterflies in his stomach every time he drove that Jeep.

A few weeks later, Andy could not take it any longer and quit.

Chapter Fifteen

Our Buick Dealership

In the 1970s Bobby had been informed there was a 1 acre parcel of land adjacent to NADE - National Automobile Dealers Exchange, the site of the largest auto auction in the world.

Bobby had asked me to be a partner in this parcel of land that I felt had little or no commercial value, so I refused. I could see no advantage in acquiring the entire parcel of land. Bobby said the price was $26,000 and the seller would take back the mortgage. I still refused for I was seeking investments that interested me and this did not.

After much arm-twisting followed by his statement "Jesus Christ, Gene, any time you have an idea I go with it. Please let's buy this land together." I reluctantly agreed and for several years we offered it for sale with no takers.

Bobby then wanted to open up an automobile reconditioning facility on that site - and once again I wanted to back off. I could not see an advantage, primarily since the parcel was too

Our Buick Dealership

small to facilitate a large enough building with ample parking even at 20,000 square feet.

Bobby spent quite a long time with my accountant to put together a pro forma statement [*financial statement*] with figures that he pulled out of the air. It might have been a good idea, however the parcel could not hold the amount of vehicles needed to be profitable.

Together, with the accountant and the builder, the total amount needed exceeded $300,000. It would be foolish - however I went along with the charade believing that no bank would finance the transaction.

At a meeting in Bordentown with representatives from the Mid-Jersey Bank, we discussed the merits of the reconditioning plant. During that meeting, a real estate agent, Jack, called me over to the side of the room and told me that the Buick agency next-door was for sale and that he thought it could be purchased for about the same money. It was situated on 5 acres and it was totally built out. I told him to immediately excuse himself from the meeting and put in an urgent call to the owner as soon as possible.

After our meeting with the bank concluded with no definitive response, I met with Ethel Forsythe. Tom Forsythe, had just died from a heart attack, which he suffered while hunting in Potter County Pennsylvania. He left a wife, Ethel and two children. Ethel was Tom's bookkeeper and now had the responsibility of running this very small agency. They were selling about 7 cars a month and there were virtually no profits

Lemon Juice

made in the past several years. The dealership provided them with Tom's salary and cars for the family's use, but that's about all. It was truly a "Mom-and-Pop" agency.

The asking price was $500,000, which I felt was ridiculously overpriced. In my estimation it was probably worth between $350,000 or possibly $375,000 at the most, but nowhere near their asking price.

I tried to rent it from her after finding out she was considering renting it to her manager for only $1,200 a month. She was talked out of it by her attorney.

After lengthy discussions and an inventory count, I offered $250,000 outright. I didn't have the money, but I had to start somewhere. It turned out, there was someone from Virginia who wanted to make the purchase for $400,000. However, he needed approval from General Motors Financing, which was a lengthy process; not something that could be done overnight and Mrs. Forsythe wanted to facilitate a deal quickly.

Her attorney called to apprise me that they had another offer, however, he never mentioned the amount. I told him all the disadvantages of paying anymore but agreed to pay the brokers fee and raised my offer to $255,101. I did this because if they had another offer and it was near mine, the additional $5,000 might place me above that other offer. I was foolish but I did not want to raise my offer above $255,101 at that time for fear they might have asked for even more. I held fast at that amount and convinced my real estate agent that this was my

Our Buick Dealership

firm and final offer. Either they take the deal or not - and their answer had to be immediate.

They contacted her attorney who was not forceful in either direction to persuade Ethel. They called the auto dealers organization for advice. They were advised to contact their legal counsel in Edison, New Jersey, attorney Mr. Davis. He met with them to discuss their needs and had called us to their Buick agency. He tried in vain to get us to increase our offer - and then said to Mrs. Forsythe "I believe that these fellows are sincere and this is a valid offer. If you want to be done with it, then sign now." She agreed and left with a $10,000 deposit. The transaction was subject to our obtaining a mortgage in the amount of $200,000 along with the proper approval from the Buick Motor Division.

The bank would approve the deal for many reasons. They thought we could generate business for the bank with them while having several accounts with business people that were certainly more aggressive than the Forsythes. They also believed that we were making an excellent purchase and because her attorney was the head of the bank and was Mrs. Forsythe's lawyer, the transaction would be concluded quickly. The bank approval came immediately.

Now for Buick: In order to obtain a new car approval from the manufacturer, many applications had to be filled out along with letters of recommendation of the individuals applying ie: to reveal any shady past. This procedure took approximately 60 days. Once I got a taste of being a Buick dealer, I could not wait the traditional 60 day period.

Lemon Juice

When Buick requested another form to be filled out, I quickly signed the papers. I drove 30 miles to the zone office and immediately completed the requested information and handed it to them personally. This occurred several times, but it saved valuable time by eliminating having to send documents in the mail.

The application was presented with both my name and Bobby's name. This is something that we have always done. However, Buick and General Motors only permitted one person as being the **dealer**. The other person was simply an 'investor.' It did not make any difference to us. Bobby was to operate our Northeast Autorama Mazda agency while I would operate the new Buick store. I had many conversations with Buick's zone manager. He was impressed with my obvious enthusiasm while being glad to see that the deal in Bordentown was being resolved.

Everything seemed to be going along smoothly. Bobby and I went to the zone office for our final operating papers. I had signed as the 'owner, operator,' while Bobby signature was only required as an 'investor.' I was happy as could possibly be to finally be the approved "dealer." This did not last for long.

A couple of days later I received a call from the dealer zone manager, Thomas Keller. "Gene, I have a problem and must speak to you in person." Within minutes I was on my way to King of Prussia, PA to Buick's zone office. He told me that he signed me as the dealer too quickly and that he received a call from headquarters in Flint, Michigan with some additional questions. They told him to hold up on the approval until they

Our Buick Dealership

received some additional information. He was bothered by this for he already had given me approval and the documents. It turned out that a very large Buick dealer in Philadelphia, had called him many times trying to get that agency for someone else. He tried to break my balls. Thomas Keller brushed aside the dealer's comments, yet they went right to the top. This dealer used their many years as a prosperous Buick dealer to put pressure on Flint, MI.

They responded by putting a hold on the approval until they gave it their blessings. This prompted zone manager Mr. Keller to request both Bobby and I accompany him to meet Buick's main man, Mr. Davis. Within a couple of hours we were airborne heading to Flint, Michigan. Mr. Keller had *strongly* requested we NOT mention that he had already given us the approval for the dealership. He felt this information might put his job in jeopardy.

Once we arrived at Flint, we were chauffeur driven to the plant where the corporate offices were located. There we were escorted into the office as Mr. Keller followed behind. I then had an entirely different opinion about him. When I first met Tom Keller - and many times thereafter - he impressed me as a forceful person who commanded the ship with an iron hand. His subordinates disliked this toughness about him, yet, it seemed very efficient to me. Here we were in Flint, Michigan, where he was totally out of his element. He seemed to be just like anyone of his subordinates. I guess that's what life is like in corporate hierarchy.

Lemon Juice

The head of the Buick's division was very congenial. He asked me the name of the Buick Dealership that I had suggested. I told him that it was to be **"Minuteman Buick."** He did **not** like that name! I gave him all the reasons that I thought it would work. I wanted to capitalize on quick service, a porter dressed in a Revolutionary War costume, while attending the showroom door. Mr. Davis again expressed his dislike for our suggested dealership's name. He pressed the issue further. This is where Bobby took command of the situation. He told Mr. Davis that he didn't like the name either. He said that years ago when we opened our first used car lot, the name was "Gene Roberts" which was a conglomeration of our first names.

Davis smiled and said **"I like it!!"** We told him that 'Gene Roberts' would be the name of the Buick dealership. Yes, "Gene Roberts Buick" it has 'verve' - and with a motion to Keller, Buick's zone manager: "You have the papers for them to sign, Keller?" "I do sir," he replied. "Well then, sign them up."

We all breathed a sigh of relief. The name was now suddenly fine with Davis. He gave it his personal 'seal of approval,' which was his way of showing us that HE commanded everything.

He could suppress flak from the local Buick dealer and others that might be bitching, since by that time every automobile dealer knew how aggressive we were. They feared competition. We returned home victorious as **Buick dealers!**

Chapter Sixteen

Where's The Money?

The next item on the agenda was to get our financing approval for the acquisition of automobiles which is called 'dealer floor planning.' We had dropped off a set of completed applications to GMAC in Trenton, New Jersey, thinking that the approval from Buick insured automatic financing through GMAC. Obviously, it was not as simple as we had expected. Each department in the General Motors family functioned separately - yet together.

The purchase price was $255,101.00 which included 5 acres of ground, a 12,000 square foot building, a Chevrolet tow truck in mint condition, some electronic tune-up machines, $9,000 in parts, plus complete office furnishings. We had both mustered together a total of $80,000. I came up with $40,000 by placing mortgages on real estate that I owned in Potter County, Pennsylvania. Bobby got his with stock holdings. Subtracting the $55,001 which we put up in cash, the bank would hold the mortgage for $200,000. All terms of the agreement had been met so we proceeded with the settlement.

Lemon Juice

To meet GMAC's minimum cash on hand requirement for floor planning we had to show that we had at least $40,000 in additional cash. The next day I brought the deposit slip to GMAC's office in Trenton and showed it to them. The final papers were then drawn up and the floor planning would be processed.

After nearly one week we were sitting in the showroom without cars. I could not purchase anything for floor planning until the final papers were approved by Buick. I used every last dollar to purchase four cars with cash. Four cars did not help the outward appearance of our new agency, so I placed them on the grass in front of the showroom facing Route 68. At least people driving by could see some semblance of life outside the dealership.

I had employees place their cars on the front lawn neatly in place making it appear that they were for sale. One vehicle I purchased from my Mazda agency was to be used as a runner between both of our locations. It was a 1969 Ford two door hardtop. I paid our Mazda agency $700.00 for it and by the end of the week sold it for $1,500. That was the first profit for our new agency.

The following week our floor planning was approved. Tom Keller had promised that he would 'pick the cherries' for my first supply of cars. That meant that he would give me more than my fair share of sharp looking fast-moving Buicks. This he did. All 26 of them were sharp, however there turned out to be one not so little drawback. Because a person in car distribution was friendly with my competitors, they gave me sharp cars alright, but they all were Buick V6s. That wasn't the best selling engine they had ever made. Looking to make the most of it, I placed a large newspaper advertisement "Gene Roberts Buick: the only Buick dealer with $400,000 worth of Buick's new Super-V6 engine!" I figured I'd turn this into a positive event.

A former partner of mine from the Estate Liquidators, Tony Russell, had agreed to be my manager. I would pay him $500 per week, Blue Cross Health Insurance and a new Buick demo to use.

Outside the showroom door was a large boulder of anthracite. It was brought to the agency as a memento of the Forsythes from their private hometown in Pennsylvania.

The morning following the hiring of Tony Russell, I found him sitting on the rock with his head resting on his hands while he was bent over leaning on his knees. He looked like a skinny Rodin in a state of depression. I asked him if he was feeling okay. He simply told me that it will be a hard job making business on these less than an active roads. I certainly did not need anyone to be depressed since he was just starting out.

As the activity began, I was getting into things. I ran promotions offering free gasoline with any test drive along with free car washes. When the mooches came simply to get a free car wash, we brought their car back and had a porter wash it. This would take time and at least give the appearance of somebody walking around the showroom looking at cars. As anyone in business knows the old adage: 'activity begets activity.'

Lemon Juice

The showroom now looked active with five sparkling new cars for sale and customers contemplating purchasing them.

Tony would take the T.O.s. That means when the salesman had a customer and could not make a deal, it would be required to 'turn over' the customer to one of his superiors. This would work to wear down a customer's resistance and hopefully lead to a better deal, if not just a deal. Tony constantly told me that to sell cars in this area you'd have to take smaller profits or else you will lose a deal altogether. I told him to stop asking for small profits and giving discounts. I explained that I made more fucking money from my house selling shit than he was presenting to me. Every time he would bring me a mini-deal, I would send him back for more. He would ask "how much more?" I would reply "as much as possible." Less than two weeks later I threw him out.

I placed advertisements for hard-hitting sales managers and started interviewing potential candidates. After hiring a few that lasted a week or two I came across Steve. I liked him. He was about 5'9" and weighed about 160 pounds. He could not only speak well, but he commanded everyone's attention when he spoke. He spoke with authority. Steve was a good T.O. man. I gave him a percentage of the bottom line with a guaranteed salary. Between the two of us jumping in on our salesmen, the profits kept growing.

The area where our new Buick agency was located was clustered with many working farms producing fruits, vegetables and raising dairy cattle. They were never used to hard-hitting salesman and it showed. When the average customer walked into our showroom looking for a new Buick, you could tell that they were unaware of our 'big city' tactics. They liked to walk slowly, talk slowly, made up their minds very slowly. I could not take this laid back wait-and-see attitude. Steve and I would converge on potential customers. The salesmen would find out the model that they wanted and bring them into Steve's office. Between Steve and myself, we performed like surgeons. We open them up. It might take five or ten minutes for us to have the customers tell us the real reasons for their hesitation and then we would know exactly what it would take to make a deal happen right then.

My salespeople, both male and female would take orders from customers along with a deposit and place the order for the car. First of all, most of the time it would take between two weeks to six weeks for the new car to arrive - but why? Why take an order when all this time we had something in stock that our customers could take home with them immediately. It might not be the same exact color or the equipment they wanted, but it was a car they could be driving right now. I would say to my salespeople "Are you assholes? Don't you realize that everyday that a car sits here in inventory that's not sold, costs me interest? Nobody leaves here without driving home in a car whether it be new or used. Sell what we have - not what is going to be built."

Momentum was picking up steadily. Each month we were making the overhead quicker than the month before. Within a three month period of time, our new car sales were higher than the agency previously had in a full year of business. The

Lemon Juice

profit per unit broke records in our Buick zone amongst over 100 dealers and finally we became the highest grossing profit dealership per unit in the country.

This led to being asked if I wanted to run for dealer representative for all US dealers in the New Jersey area. Usually one or two votes out of a potential 25 was enough to win. It seems as though most dealers previously voted for themselves and the one that had one or two friends, convinced them to vote in their favor. That wasn't good enough for me. I called my zone manager and asked him if he thought it would do me any good being elected. He thought it would add some prestige to our agency.

The next morning I had my secretary get the phone numbers of every dealer in my area. I called each one telling them that I already had five votes which was more than enough to win. However, to be most effective for the group, I would like them and their friends to vote for me so it would be unanimous. I expressed concerns for better relations with the factory and with their full support the factory would listen to our concerns. I received 22 votes.

Tom Keller had called requesting that I purchase a new Buick 4 foot stretch limousine made by a company they wanted me to do business with. He said that he was asked by the head of Buick division to have one limousine in each Buick zone. Not hesitating a moment I asked "any particular color in mind?"

Within six weeks my new Buick Silver Hawk limousine was delivered from Fort Smith, Arkansas. The unit was drop-shipped from the plant in Flint, Michigan where it was produced, to Fort Smith, Arkansas for conversion into a limousine. I ordered it in silver gray with crushed blue velour interior. The color match where the car was stretched at the center was poor. There was a noticeable difference in the shade of gray. I admit that I am particular but others also noticed it. The price for the conversion was $8,000. After two hours on the phone with the conversion company, I chopped off $3,000 and we had a less expensive limousine.

I placed the limousine ads immediately. After placing an advertisement in some newspapers for a chauffeur, I started hiring. I had gone through two chauffeurs within one week. Neither one knew their way around and both had drawbacks. The first was nearly deaf which necessitated lowering the glass partition so I could shout directions while the other usually was drunk and could not understand directions. Luckily, the following week I hired Ron.

Ron was the perfect chauffeur. He dressed in a smart gray suit and always wore handmade bowties. Ron was almost bald with the center of his head looking like a spit shine. He was no taller than 5' 5" and had a slight build. He was intelligent, having been a bookkeeper and an antique dealer in the past.

Why he wanted this job, which paid only $100 a week, was a mystery to me. Within the week he was answering the phones at the agency and doing follow-up calls to customers when he wasn't driving. He was always prompt, picking me up no later than 7:30am. I gave him time off during the day but he spent much of that time hanging around the dealership. At night

Lemon Juice

he would drive me home, usually after 10 or 11 o'clock. On occasions I would send Ron with the limousine to bankers and representatives from Buick as my treat. It was very effective.

Early one morning I received a call from my shop foreman Hank. It was about 5am when he called. "Gene, there's a fire at the agency." I was startled. "How bad is it?," I inquired. "Not too bad. The firemen are here now and it's under control." I asked what were the extent of the damages. I was told by Hank that my office was burnt but everything else seemed okay. I told them that I would be in as soon as possible. I stopped at Dunkin' Donuts on my way in and got coffee and donuts for 10 people. It was not enough. By the time I arrived, there was no office. There was no shop. Only the frame of the building still existed. I looked at Hank and said "This is what you call 'not too bad'?"

The damages totaled nearly $400,000. Cars were burnt that were in the showroom and in the shop. Parts were destroyed. We were out of business… temporarily.

I gathered my thoughts together. Call the insurance company. Did we have sufficient coverage? Call this trailer rental company, get temporary lighting on this property from a lighting rental service. Hire guards to watch the empty facility. Don't let the employees panic. Call the newspapers and place an advertisement apprising the public that we are still in business.

Within hours my lawyer had called a public adjustment company. They were to itemize every nut and bolt. Everything that we were unable to identify because of seeing them for

Where's The Money?

so long. For instance a simple carpet that was between two offices. It had a replacement value of $50. Who cares? When you add them together, hundreds upon hundreds of items that you didn't take notice, they tended to add up to a sizable sum.

The adjustment company wanted 10% of the proceeds. I haggled with them until we both agreed upon 6%. After two weeks of difficult and dirty work, the figures that the adjustment company came up with exceeded $350,000. The general adjustment company that the insurance company used came up with $275,000. They made their offer firm, which I emphatically refused. Bobby wanted me to take it because we needed the money to rebuild and to capitalize the business in order to get things restarted. I played it cool. The insurance company then upped their offered to $300,000.

Bobby, along with the adjustment company, started to twist my arm to sign off on their offer. Even my lawyer told me to accept it. I still refused. It was a good offer but not good enough. I felt that I was not losing anytime because I was working with different contractors, negotiating deals to get the building back together by salvaging as much as possible.

There were a few warped beams that had to be replaced, but not all of them. I called the insurance adjuster myself. I told him I was going to sue for $1 million. The adjuster told me that he would be able to authorize additional money. After he looked at the mess of my destroyed Buick agency, we went to lunch at a diner on route 206. There at lunch, we negotiated a favorable settlement with them which brought the total proceeds to

Lemon Juice

$400,000, a full 25% more than their prior offer and from the public adjusters.

The following day I told the public adjuster that I was going to take the insurance company to court. Three hours later I settled with them for $12,000. That represented 4%. One week later a check was issued to us in the amount of $400,000 and our claim was settled.

The contractors were in a bidding war against each other and we finally contracted to repair the remains and patch up the building for $125,000. We had a surplus of cash which we used to restock the parts department and dress up the agency along with paying many bills incurred during the four months of lost operations. With our refurbished building complete we were once again in business.

At this time there was a lull in new car sales. Our inventory was overloaded with all the new downsized Buick Electra. People that were accustomed to full-size automobiles stayed away from the new Buick line. It took much in the way of promotions to get sales rolling again. I have never liked intermediate sized cars but this was a different world. The new models were smaller, yet still large enough inside affording the same comfort. They were much more economical than their forerunner, which looked like fishing boats compared to the new sleeker designs.

New car announcements came for the 1978 Buicks in mid-September of 1977. Car dealers always promoted the event doing something special to lure customers into their showrooms. I ran a newspaper advertisement that we were having a party, serving hors d'oeuvres and champagne to celebrate the arrival of the new 1978 Buicks.

Customers were wandering into the showroom with salesman and women showing the new automobiles, while being as hospitable as possible. As the clock turned 2pm, the order from the local deli brought numerous trays of mini-sandwiches. No expense was spared as one-third of the sandwiches were filet mignon on buttered pocket rolls, while the other sandwiches were traditional turkey, ham and tuna half-sandwiches.

Then about 3 o'clock in the afternoon someone else arrived toting a couple of large aluminum pans containing brownies and set them on the table along with the cookies and other assorted desserts adjoining the display of delicious sandwiches. Chilled champagne bottles were uncorked and sitting in ice buckets with four dozen flutes parked next to them and more champagne waiting in the rear office, if needed.

I took a nibble of one of the brownies but it was not like anything I had ever tasted before. They contained what appeared to look like some sort of lawn clippings mixed with chocolate. "What the hell," I said as I enthusiastically started to consume mine, figuring that the baker knew cookies and cakes and I know automobiles. Everyone has their own 'niche.'

Sales people from all departments meandered into the office, including the mechanics and bookkeepers, to enjoy the flutes of champagne and nibble on the various desserts.

Lemon Juice

I then finished my brownie, which tasted horrible. It tasted like cow manure. At that point we were running low on cookies, so people tended to eat the brownies.

I watched their faces and it was obvious that these brownies tasted like crap to everyone who ate them. Yet, after about 20 minutes or so, customers and office staff alike were gravitating toward the aluminum pans containing the brownies, taking a second and even a third helping. This was puzzling considering they tasted like shit.

Within another half-hour everything seemed to slow down. It was like watching everything in slow motion. My accountant looked like he was going to vomit when he ate the first brownie but was now reaching for more.

Our customers were in no hurry to go home. They crowded around the aluminum pans like cattle at a watering hole. Some were even jockeying for the prime position around the pans. To say the place was 'buzzing' would have been putting it mildly.

A base group leader at Fort Dix and his absolutely stunning wife who looked like a model from a fashion magazine, but had a bit of an attitude, were very interested in buying a Buick Electra. It was a 4 door in black with a burgundy crushed velour interior. It was a handsome vehicle that I had used as a demo just the day before. They each had a champagne flute in hand and brownie in the other hand when I left them in the company of a very capable saleswoman.

Where's The Money?

As I walked from one sales booth to another, checking on the salespeople and their customers, I wandered back to see if the deal had been consummated with the couple from Fort Dix. To my surprise, nobody was moving. My saleswoman was sitting at her desk with a sales order pad in one hand and was leaning on her right hand resting her head. She had fallen asleep.

The group leader and his wife were also fast asleep. "Wake up, wake up," I said not wanting to shock them, but gave them a gentle 'wake-up' nudge so they could finish signing the sales papers and drive off in their new car. At the same time I gave a gentle smack to the back of the saleswoman's head to wake her up. Within 15 minutes they were driving back to Fort Dix in their beautiful new Buick Electra.

The following day a customer who had attended the new car announcement, called asking for the name of the bakery that made the brownies since his wife loved them so much. It was sometime later, I was informed that someone had laced those brownies with pot. I wondered if our "high" sales performance that day could be attributable to the pot(?) If so, how did it ever get there and who delivered it? I never received an invoice for them; only for the sandwiches.

Chapter Seventeen

Schpeel-Kiss

In 1982, I sold a significant piece of property to U-Haul, dealing with Sam Shoen who was the owner. With the proceeds, I purchased a 42 foot Jersey sport-fishing boat that had previously been called "Special K," because the owner's surname began with the letter K. I renamed the boat "Schpeel-Kiss" [*Yiddish: Sitting on pins and needles*].

Since Yiddish is a dialect, there's no official spelling of any specific word. To come up with an acceptable spelling, I wrote variations on 3x5 index cards and proceeded to walk down the boardwalk asking people along the way to pronounce what I had written. Most of them thought I was just a total off-the-wall freaking idiot, but if they were able to say '*spiel kiss*,' then, I determined that's the way I'm going.

After a few years in 1986, I found an advertisement in one of the yachting magazines for a 1957 Pacemaker motor yacht. Price: $475,000 firm. It was described as being in 'magnificent condition,' and with only 200 hours. I was greatly interested in following up. I contacted the owner, Joe Carigole, a wealthy

Schpeel-Kiss

businessman, of the yacht known as "Star Liner" to arrange an appointment to see this yacht. At that time Marlene and I still owned the 42 foot Jersey sport fishing boat, "Schpeel-Kiss." We felt the 57 foot yacht "Star Liner" would give us the extra room that we desired.

Shortly after speaking with the owner, we drove to Maryland and viewed the boat docked at the Baltimore Inner Harbor Marina.

The owner had arranged to have his captain take me for a test drive. During the drive I notice there was a vibration at two different speeds which indicated possibly bad driveshafts or propellers that were out of balance. Either one could run into the thousand to repair.

The owner indicated that he would take care of the vibration. I had made him an offer of $375,000 cash - no financing, no trade; a quick, easy sale. He refused, telling me that he had a lot of responses from the advertisement in the yachting magazine and that the following week someone was coming from either Connecticut or Massachusetts to inspect the boat at the full price. I felt that he was full of crap and that I was his best and possibly only potential purchaser.

I told him that I would give him a few days to accept my offer or else I would walk away and likely purchase something else - or just keep my boat. I did receive a call from him stating he would take $425,000 which was still $50,000 over my offer. I stuck to my guns at $375,000. I called back to find out if he

Lemon Juice

had the work done for the driveshafts and propellers and I wanted him to guarantee there was no vibration.

The next thing I remember is that I received a call from an attorney that represented him stating that he'll sell me the boat for the $375,000 "as is." I agreed, but wanted it in writing that there was no more vibration. I tried to call the seller personally but he was becoming more and more unavailable and I was getting concerned that possibly he had another customer.

I got back in touch with his lawyer since the owner was not being made available and said 'you have a deal for the $375,000.' The lawyer wanted to know how much I would give him as a deposit to purchase the yacht. I told him to send me an agreement of sale and I would send him $50,000 as a deposit. We would cash up the deal immediately.

The attorney sent me an agreement of sale and said that Joe Carigole, the owner, was selling me the yacht for the sum of $1.00 receipt of which he hereby acknowledged. I could not believe what I was reading. I didn't have to pay a penny! Well, actually a dollar is what I would have to pay and I could have forced the sale. I wouldn't do that. I wanted the yacht.

To purchase the yacht, I would have had to pay 6% sales tax. However, if I traded my Jersey sport fishing boat, which I had a customer for $150,000, I could subtract that from the $375,000, reducing the tax, providing the purchaser of my Jersey boat would be willing to physically meet in Delaware where the entire transaction would be closed.

Schpeel-Kiss

The seller of the yacht was having seller's remorse. He did not want to go through with the deal. I called his lawyer and told him that I already had an agreement of sale signed by the seller and witnessed by the attorney who represented the seller. If they gave me any crap and would not cooperate by completing the deal where and when I wanted, I would force the issue for the $1.00 paid-in-full bill of sale received and witnessed. They both realized that they screwed up and then became reluctantly cooperative.

We gathered at a restaurant off of Rt 95 in Delaware and completed the deal. My boat was sold for $150,000 and the seller showed it was being traded and he was selling it to my buyer.

The boat was docked at the Baltimore Inner Harbor. I read up about Loran Navigation Systems (the predecessor of GPS). Marlene and I took a local navigation course. Since I never had a boat this large, I hired the owner's captain to deliver the boat to Atlantic City. He was at the controls as we exited the inner coast crossing the Delaware Bay when I told him to stop. I screamed **STOP the fucking boat!** According to my Loran, he was heading into 2 feet of water when my new yacht drew a tad over 4 feet. I had him back up and then I took over the controls. By the way, Hurricane Andrew was one hour behind us heading our way, so we had to make time. Pulling into Atlantic City Marina (later to be known as Trump's Castle Marina), the pilings were only 18 feet apart. My new yacht was 17½ feet wide and there were wind gusts up to 65 mph. I really don't know how I did it, but I managed to moor the

Lemon Juice

boat exactly between the two pilings. My reflexes were sharp and so I pulled in and tied up without any damage. Later that evening, Hurricane Andrew struck and blew the Bimini top off my boat.

Now we go to Atlantic City the morning after Hurricane Andrew hit. An imported trawler from Connecticut pulled in during the storm for shelter, literally one boat from where I was docked. The boat had a white hull with a wide blue band. I was standing on the pier looking over what we had just brought through the storm to see if there was any damage that I hadn't noticed, when the fellow yachtsman was also looking at his boat taking strange looks at my boat.

He saw the name "Star Liner" and asked me if this was my boat or was it Joe Carigole's? He almost passed out when I told him that I just purchased the boat. He was the customer who offered $75,000 more for the boat, which the seller was waiting for and that is why the seller kept procrastinating. I could have sold him the boat right then and there and made a handsome profit, but that boat was not for sale. Not then.

We renamed the yacht the "Formal Affair" and took it to New England and the Bahamas, just the two of us. We nearly died crossing the Gulf Stream when we were hit by two storms. The powerful waves soared over the top of my bridge by 24 feet!

I advertised in the Atlantic City Press for a part-time experienced chef. I interviewed a few people and one was Jimmy. He was Ivanna and Donald Trump's chef and was on call 24 hours a day for Japanese high-rollers that wanted excellent food.

Schpeel-Kiss

He worked for us from about 5 o'clock to 7 o'clock, along with his wife, who served and cleaned up.

Jimmy told me that Donald only eats steak and wasn't particular about how the steak was prepared. Whereas, Ivana had excellent culinary taste. Jimmy was the chef who introduced me to sashimi.

My next-door neighbor had an ocean yacht Sport-Fishing boat. He was out sport fishing all the time and gave me a couple pounds of prime tuna filet.

I gave the piece of tuna to Jimmy, who sliced it and made a wasabi sauce, he asked me taste it. That was my first experience eating raw fish. To thank the people next door who gave me the fish, I had a platter made and bought it next door to the fishermen. They thanked me but said they only eat steak and hated fish.

We were hosting a party on the Formal Affair. Some celebrities from Trump's Castle and Marina were on board as my guests. The head [*toilet*] in the master bedroom was used by someone and became clogged. I inserted a plunger that worked on pressure, feeling that it would clear the line, without realizing it only expanded the line that was to head overboard. When I released the line, the shit literally hit the fan. Everything that was in there blew through the toilet, covering the walls, floor, ceiling and carpeting. It made me realize, one can have all the titles and riches in the world, but when crap gets all over everything, you aren't much different than any other person having to deal with a shitty problem.

Lemon Juice

In the fall of 1986, we decided to take a trip on the "Formal Affair" to spend the winter in Florida. I never met a boat owner from the northern part of United States who did not dream of someday taking their boat to Florida for the winter, or as Palm Beachers put it "Wintering in Florida."

I hired a Captain that delivered yachts for a major yacht company and figured that he would educate me about the use of my new electronic equipment and navigation system. At that time GPS was being used solely by the government and Loran was used by the general public, but it was not as precise as GPS. I believe that was a security concern even though eventually GPS transformed into what it is today.

Bob, the captain, was a pleasant enough person about 6 feet tall, black hair, of slender build, approximately 40 years old. His fee for navigating the boat to Palm Beach was $1.000, plus food and board. And of course airfare back home.

The first day that we met him was in the afternoon. We had planned to take off at sunrise the following morning. Bob slept in the full berth while my wife and I enjoyed the ultra comfort in the master stateroom with its built-in king-size bed.

Early the following morning we said goodbye to the few people that were awake at the pier, untied the mooring lines and headed to the Hamptons in Virginia.

Bob had a little packet that he used for navigation purposes. He opened it up and basically said from point A to point B is 175 miles and that is the degree in which to head. This seemed strange to me. Being a novice, I wondered why he did not program my Loran, but I soon found out why. He never used one. This was incredible. I hired a boat captain that delivers million dollar yachts and he didn't know how to use the electronics, especially the one specifically designed for navigation.

On our trip from Baltimore Inner Harbor, where my boat was kept prior to my acquisition, I had taught myself the fundamentals of the Loran system, but I certainly was not an expert. I had Bob stay at the helm station and follow the compass heading towards Virginia. While he held a course, I started reading up as much as I could and as quickly as possible to absorb the instructions. I needed to understand how to enter information as accurately as possible. Within a couple hours, I was able to pinpoint within approximately 75 foot accuracy where we were positioned and where we were heading.

The weather was less than ideal. It was raining and according to the radar it was pretty heavy where we were heading. That evening we pulled up to the marina in Virginia and as the captain handed me the steering wheel he said he would get the boat lines 'tied up.' "Wait a minute," I said. "You expect **me** to maneuver this boat into the narrow slip that is barely visible?" Before he could answer I took a hold of the controls and was maneuvering this 80,000 pound displacement yacht perfectly into position as Bob tied the lines. "Whew!" It was quite the nerve-racking experience, but on the good side of the coin, I was gaining experience.

The rest of the navigation was basically from point A to point B, not being concerned with heavy waves and the uncertainty

Lemon Juice

of the ocean. In the meantime, even though it was not a major feat to navigate the Intracoastal Waterway, there was much one had to beware of. I had to constantly make sure the boat did not drift out of the channel, nor hit bottom, which could damaged the propellers, rendering the boat not only useless, but a chore to have it pulled out of the water for major repairs.

There were countless bridges on our trip south, many of which required contacting the bridge operator requesting an opening. Our boat was 25 feet tall at its highest point, so we constantly had to be aware of how much overhead distance there was so that we did not cause damage.

Many times there was a half-hour wait for a bridge to open, however coming into South Carolina I had an idea. I opened the cabinet that held our life preservers, remembering there was a Confederate flag stowed there from the previous owner - for what purpose, I had no idea. I put it on the bow, replacing the flag I had custom made for our yacht. I told Marlene to take a pillow and put it under her blouse to make it appeared that she was pregnant. I called on the ship-to-shore radio using a very southern accent and told the bridge tender that I had the governor's daughter on board who was pregnant and I had to take her to her destination as quickly as possible. I never said where. I didn't even know who the governor was. The bridge operator apprised me that she would oblige as quickly as possible - and she did. I asked her for her name so that I could tell the governor how cooperative she was. That little deception opened up lots of bridges for us and made our trip somewhat quicker.

Schpeel-Kiss

We eventually made it to the marina in North Palm Beach and tied up with no problem. A couple hours later, after Bob and I washed the boat, he came to me to be paid. I handed him the money in cash. He said "I never learned so much about navigation and operating this equipment as I did on this trip! I want to thank you so much for this experience." My stomach churned as I handed him the money. Here I am paying him to teach **me** and wound up teaching **him** - plus I had to pay for the privilege! I never hired another boat captain again! From that point forward, my wife and I navigated our yacht through storms that killed people! We had taken the boat as far north as Boston, Massachusetts and as far south as the Bahamas.

We were welcomed at Old Port Cove where we planned to stay the winter, but that did not happen.

Our boat slip was at the foremost prominent location at Old Port Cove. Everyday those on their casual exercise mode would walk the cement 'trail' that encompassed the entire complex of condominium towers.

Old Port Cove had two drawbacks: First it was not deemed to be a 'hurricane hole' which meant during a hurricane all boats would have to leave their moorings to seek shelter. The second, which was just as important, was where we were docked were all the 'Yentas' [*Yiddish for story tellers that cannot keep a secret*], who walked by our boat everyday seeking some conversation. We were a relatively young couple compared to the residents, which became a focal point of discussion. Mostly: 'What did he do for a living that they can spend the winter here on their own yacht?'

Chapter Eighteen

$700 a Knight

Marlene and I became friendly with Jerry and his beautiful young wife Cathy. Jerry had been to Florida numerous times and owned a lovely sport fishing boat. Jerry was a major importer of items from China that one always finds in gift shops. He invited us to a party that was held almost weekly at Old Port Cove. There, we were introduced as the new arrivals which put us in the center of everyone's discussions, since the majority of them were totally bored living out their retirement in Florida.

The head of the condo association was a Col. Edward Neilson, who turned out to be a good friend of my former partner Bobby Gordon. Col. Neilson invited Marlene and I to party after party.

The rumors were plentiful about my source of income. Why? Who the hell knows? I was a diversion for their boredom.

One day I received a call from my new friend Jerry to tell me that at the latest party he attended, someone told him that

$700 a Knight

I must be a drug dealer. He asked me emphatically if that's what I was.

I was shocked and responded that whoever mentioned that was terrible for spreading such a malicious rumor. He then told me it was his friend Howard. Having enough with all these yentas, I placed a phone call to Howard. I asked him if he was really the source of these rumors that I was a drug dealer? If so, he should be scared for his life! A few minutes later he was rushed to the hospital. It seems as he got a panic attack while he was in the bathroom taking a pee and collapsed, falling into the toilet that he was peeing in. As a result, he broke his shoulder.

No one mentioned this to me. At the next party - there was Howie at the bar having a drink. I walked up to him ordered a kamikaze and put my arm around his back and gave him a squeeze while whispering in his ear. "You'll never know for sure." He screamed in pain, which scared the heck out of me since I did not know what had happened to him after my phone call.

About a week later the dock master came to visit me on my boat. He said that Old Port Cove does not permit dogs. Prior to our heading to Florida I informed the person with whom I signed the contract that I had a 70 pound white poodle named "Shalom." I told him to get back in touch with the people that I signed the contract with. In the meantime, I was disillusioned being in the midst of the Super Bowl of Yentas and was looking for a safer place, especially since a hurricane was due to hit Florida.

Lemon Juice

A couple of miles north of Old Port Cove we found a very private marina that housed about 75 boats. I came to an agreement with the owner of the marina who had full knowledge of my dog and I wound up purchasing the boat slip. The facility was called "The Bluffs." It was surrounded with low-rise condos and was a perfect hurricane hole. Within the week I was out of Old Port Cove and moved into The Bluffs.

Reading the local newspaper, I found an article about piano concerts held weekly on Sundays in Palm Beach at the Ocean Grande Hotel, which shortly would become a Four Seasons Hotel. We attended our first concert and was very impressed with the music of pianists that were tuning themselves up for the soon-to-be Palm Beach International Piano Competition.

The concerts were held in a small quiet area of the hotel which also had a bar so I could have my kamikazes while reclining in a very cushioned chair. I seriously enjoyed this experience so much so that I tracked down the organizer, John Bryan, to thank him for putting this together. After the second Sunday, I went to speak to John to find out what I could do to help him, especially due to both Marlene and my love of music. John told me that he was on a tight budget and was having difficulty getting paying patrons. That was right up my alley since I've been marketing all my life. I informed him then I would gladly help.

I typed up discount cards to be handed out which stated "Two-For-One. Buy one ticket to a Sunday afternoon concert and bring a friend for free." It was easy. I just doubled the $10 entry fee to $20.00 and then went to every McDonald and

$700 a Knight

Burger King that I could find and handed out stacks of these discount coupons. I told John that I also printed discount cards that would give them 50% off their next visit to the concerts.

Two weeks later all hell broke loose. "Where can we get enough seats for everyone that's coming?" The owner of the hotel was complaining that there were too many people wanting to attend. So from a concert that was losing money, fourteen days later they didn't know how to handle everyone that was attending!

Sometimes you just can't win - but I didn't accept that. I told the owner that their bar business will pick up greatly as long as they give them a discount which I would offer all those that attend. Two weeks later the bar was busy and the facility did not have room for one more chair.

I enjoyed the concert and the piano competition so much that I eventually authorized an oil painting of the pianist seated at a concert grand piano performing on the beach with waves lapping at the pianist's feet. Surprisingly everyone that looked at the painting wondered how did I ever move such an expensive piano onto the beach. People can really be dumb.

Before I realized it, everyone was thanking me for helping the Palm Beach International Piano Competition pay its bills and even show a profit. I contacted the local newspapers asking them to attend so that they could show a packed audience. This usually perpetuates more audience, which it did.

Lemon Juice

John introduced us to some Cuban friends of his that recently opened up a restaurant In the area. Before I knew It, I was involved helping to promote their new restaurant.

Both Marlene and I liked John and his male partner Winston, who was a designer and very good at his work. We would socialize together and wound up being at more and more parties together. It was like networking before the computer age.

Each year Palm Beach held the "Byzantine Ball." It was THE highlight event in Palm Beach. Major sponsors of the Palm Beach International Piano Competition plus an untold amount of locals signed up to attend. No one wanted to miss it since Prince Henri of Malta and the Princess would always be there for photo ops. I believe that John Bryan and his organization paid for the Prince and Princess to stay at an exclusive hotel in the heart of Palm Beach.

John and I became personal friends and he constantly inquired about what I did and my interest in helping out others. I received a call from someone who claimed to be representing Prince Henri Constantine and was asking about my background, since they heard about me and what I was doing to help out John Bryan and the Guild for International Piano Competition. He asked permission to contact some of the organizations back home that I had helped. Shortly after, I received another call asking if I could attend a ceremony at a Greek Orthodox Church in Palm Beach. I asked why? He responded by saying that both my wife and I were to be honored by Prince Henri Constantine and Princess Françoise Paleologo of Malta with a Knighthood.

$700 a Knight

At that time my mother had come to visit us on our yacht to spend ten days before heading home. I believe she was 86 years old and looked like she was in her early sixties. But there was a hook in bestowing Knighthood to both my wife and myself. I was told that a woman was honored as a Countess for donating $50,000. A local lawyer for a $25,000. They wanted to know what I could donate. I told them **zero**. I would have nothing to do with being Knighted if it was based solely on how much I donated to them. I told the person that called on behalf of the Prince and Princess that I only donate to organizations that I have personally vetted. I would donate to the local Greek Orthodox Church; but not to the Knights of Malta.

The Prince and Princess asked for the sum of $1,400 to be donated to the Greek Orthodox Church. I told them that is their choice. It made no difference to me. He told me that he was so glad to speak with me and to understand where I was coming from as opposed to all those people that paid to be Knighted.

To me, that contribution came out of the $700 a night. It was $300 just to attend the Byzantine Ball, which turned out to be in my honor and a big surprise! Yes, I was Knighted along with my wife, Marlene. I looked handsome, if I may say so myself, in my black tuxedo and my standard bearer, a Victorian walking stick with gold handle. Everyone was coming over to congratulate both my wife, now "Dame Marlene," and myself, "Sir Eugene" - a Knight.

Lemon Juice

When I look back over the course of my life, I've certainly come a long way since those days when I was making address signs and repairing bicycles.

I vividly remember the ceremony when Prince Henri placed his sword on my shoulder and stated: "**Be valiant.**" Reflecting on that motto, I feel it actually made me concentrate even more on helping others. It became rewarding to a greater extent for me to improve the quality of the lives of others, rather than merely having a good time in life for myself.

I was very much influenced by both my mother and father when it came to helping those in need. My maternal grandparents were the best example for they had very little financially, yet they gave everything they could to those who had less than them.

On my maternal grandmother's side of the family, the Axelrods were extremely well off as they were industrialists. Shortly after my father died, I was invited to the opening of my mother's cousin George Sall's precious metals plant at Tulip and Westmoreland in the Tacony section of North Philadelphia. They just opened their new plant (I believe in 1951 it cost approximately $11 million).

My cousin, Bobby and I were escorted through George's new plant and then he handed both of us a new aluminum ingot. After that he invited us into his gorgeous office where he sat behind his huge desk. I will never forget the conversation. I remember him receiving a telephone call which George took while we sat there.

$700 a Knight

During the conversation, he opened a file box and fingered through the various 3x5 index cards, pulling one out of the box. "Yes. Don't worry, I will take care of it now." I heard him say. After the brief conversation, George told me what was in the index box. "There will always be people in need - and **you** should always do your best to help." The box was jammed full of index cards pertaining to people that he was helping financially. I took his advice to heart.

Chapter Nineteen

Have a Heart?

Upon eating a sumptuous meal at the Blue Bell Inn and enjoying their incredible fried oysters, followed by a fillet mignon smothered with béarnaise sauce and finishing the dinner with dessert, only a few hours passed when my brother, Wesley, suffered yet another heart attack.

I was notified by my brother, Mickey (Milton). We both rushed to the hospital. My brother, Wesley, was on life support. This has been his eighth heart attack. At least two occurred within hours of having a festive dinner.

Wesley looked terrible and his prognosis was dire. His personal physician told me that only 9% of his heart was functioning and that I should say my goodbyes to my brother.

Wesley was a veteran serviceman who fought in World War II. At 18 years of age, he joined the United States Army Air Force. He envisioned himself as the 'Red Baron.' After extensive training, he was to receive news that was a great disappointment to him. He, along with over 3,000 other new pilots, were needed in the infantry. Their group was washed out of the Air Corp. His new group was the 63rd "Blood and Fire" division.

One day we received word that he got a two day pass, left Fort Bragg in North Carolina and headed home. We waited anxiously for his arrival. The day seemed to get longer and longer, but an hour or two after it got dark he was at the front door. I remember sitting on the carpeted steps to the second floor when the door opened. Everybody rushed over to give Wesley hugs and kisses. He then turned around to his left, saw me perched on the stairs and came running over. He grabbed me under my arms as he gave his kid brother hugs and kisses. My handsome warrior brother wanted to greet his little 'pisher' brother first!

His time at home flew by quickly and before long he was fighting on the front in Germany. In one fierce battle, he spent 17 days in a foxhole seeing many of his comrades killed. Wesley never said a thing about what happened, nor what he witnessed in the years he spent in the service. It wasn't until his passing that his son, Scott, found papers which Wesley wrote describing what he saw as one of the first liberators of the concentration camps. Those papers that he originally typed, have been requested by the Philadelphia Holocaust Museum.

Not being satisfied after speaking with my brother's physician, I also met with the head of cardiology at Holy Redeemer Hospital. "Gene, you must accept the fact that your brother will be gone in 24 hours. If he had terminal cancer you would understand it better," the doctor had said to me. I responded "Is there nothing that can be done to save his life? Can we get him a heart transplant? We have to do something," were just some of my questions that seemed to fall on deaf ears. "No surgeon will perform a heart transplant on your brother. He's not a good candidate for a transplant. For one thing, he's too old at 63 and for another thing..." I interrupted him right there... "Fuck you both! I'm not giving up. If there's a way to get him a heart - I will do it!!"

It was 1986, before Al Gore invented the Internet, so I had to make calls on a public pay phone to find out who heads up the organ transplant programs in hospitals around the country. Within a half-hour I had the names of Dr. Michael DeBakey at Methodist Medical Center in Houston, Texas. He was the first cardiac surgeon in the USA to perform transplants successfully. Dr. Norman Shumway at Stanford University in Palo Alto, California, Dr. Bartley Griffith at Pittsburgh Presbyterian Medical Center, and a name that I forget at Johns Hopkins in Baltimore, MD plus a doctor at Temple University.

While I was working the telephone, my brother Mickey was gathering together transcriptions of Wesley's medical records. I actually got to speak to heads of each transplant group. Temple University was the closest in proximity. My brother was transferred to Temple. I spoke with the cardiologist on the transplant team who told me that they have to perform a series of tests to see if Wesley qualifies for a transplant. "How long will these test take?" I asked, knowing full well that my brother was running out of time.

Have a Heart?

After nearly a week of Wesley being in the hospital, I was summoned to the transplant doctor's office with my brother Mickey. The test results were exactly the same as the test results performed at the previous hospital. "I'm sorry, but we're not going to be able to perform a transplant for your brother - he's too old." My brother, Mickey, trying to hold me back as I was reaching over the desk to grab the throat of that son of a bitch. My brother was only six days older than he was when he was admitted to the hospital for the tests.

Back to Holy Redeemer. In the meantime I spoke with Dr. Norman Shumway who had performed over 500 heart transplants. He told me to get in touch with Dr. Bartley Griffith at Pittsburgh Presbyterian, who had success with older patients.

Financial arrangements had to be made prior to getting my brother to Pittsburgh. Within one hour I had all the financial arrangements in place. I met with the cardiologist at Holy Redeemer informing him that Pittsburgh Presbyterian is willing to put a heart in my brother's chest. "We have to perform a Swan Ganz test [*Pulmonary artery catheterization invented by Jeremy Swan and William Ganz to test for heart failure or sepsis*] before we discharge him," he explained, as a Medevac plane was waiting for us to airlift my brother to Pittsburgh. I could not believe this. It was only a few days before that I was told there was nothing that could be done for my brother, yet now he required a test to determine his eligibility for a heart transplant.

Lemon Juice

I called Dr. Griffith in Pittsburgh who spoke with the cardiologist. Dr. Griffith told me to let him do the test, it's purely financial and that he was going to do the test anyway, not trusting anyone else's results. Ninety minutes later we were wheeling my brother on a gurney into a small propeller plane.

On May 8th 1986, only 24 hours later, my brother, Wesley, received a new heart! He lived an additional 12 years with that new heart; the last two years being difficult for him as he needed dialysis.

I was so appreciative of the fact that I was able, against all odds, to get my brother, who I loved so much, a new heart, that I wanted to give back somehow, someway.

After months of constantly having it on my mind, I designed "Project Organ Donor a Commitment for Life." United States Representative James Greenwood of the Eight Congressional District, sat in on the health committee board hearings for organ transplantation. Twelve transplant doctors around the United States testified and backed my transplant program.

I witnessed firsthand people waiting for a transplant, as well as those whose loved ones were involved in accidents and were potential organ donors. Just because your driver's license says that you are an organ donor, don't believe it. It's marketing bullshit. No hospital will take your organs without the next of kin's approval. They do not want to risk being sued by a family member who did not approve the organ donation. My program was simple: I wanted the United States

Have a Heart?

government to issue a free $10,000 life insurance policy to everyone in the country that would be payable to whoever they named as a beneficiary upon a successful organ transplant. It's basically an insurance policy that would cost the government approximately $2 per person. However, the benefits were overwhelming.

First, picture being a parent traumatized after hearing that their child has been in a tragic accident and is brain-dead. Now according to UNOS [*United Network of Organ Sharing*], someone from their organization is supposed to meet with the next of kin within one hour of this tragedy to ask them to sign off for an organ removal or "harvesting" the organ. Not only would that person be facing the trauma of first learning about their child's status, but someone else would have to be there asking them to make a decision while they could possibly be in a state of emotional shock. My program eliminated the second trauma because the insurance policy would already be in effect, as it had to be signed by not only the potential donor - but also the donor's next of kin; thus that decision would have already been made by the organ donor and the next of kin.

While nearly 100,000 people are on the organ donor waiting list, thousands die unnecessarily each year while waiting for an organ that never materializes. I received a call from Richard DeVos, the founder of Amway Products, who at the time was head of the National Chamber of Commerce and also one of the single largest donors to the Republican Party. He had received a new heart and wanted my program to go through

Congress and get approval. He met on my behalf with Dick Cheney.

Richard DeVos had given a speech in New York at the Chamber of Commerce and as soon as he finished, he met with me and my daughter, Ellen, at the famous Bull and Bear restaurant in the Waldorf-Astoria. He loved everything about my program and wanted to assure me that he would do everything he could to get support in the House and Senate.

In the meantime, another friend who was an organ recipient was able to get an actuarial firm to calculate how it would financially affect the United States government's pocketbook. To our surprise, it was not only cost efficient, but in 1988 it would have saved the government $2 billion annually. That had nothing to do with the altruistic reason for doing this. Peoples' lives would not only be saved, but it would enable many of them to be productive once again. They would be able to get back into society, working and paying taxes, instead of being unemployed, receiving disability benefits and costing up to $20,000 a month for dialysis. It seemed to be a rational approach to organ transplants and donations.

My suggested program made the national news following my presentation to Congress' Health Committee at the Rayburn building.

Epilogue

Once I was able to pay off the mortgage of my mother's home in Logan and was aware that I was making significantly more than the average wage earner, I made a conscious decision to do whatever I could, even in a small way, to help those that needed financial help the most.

It certainly wasn't difficult looking too far to find people in need. Right in front of me was my aunt Gert, who lived in a rundown neighborhood with very little income. I sent her checks on a monthly basis to subsidize her meager income until the day that she passed away. One generation down from her was her daughter. She too needed additional financial assistance. Add her to the list.

After marrying, Marlene would send out monthly checks to five people. It became a habit and the part of my 'overhead.' No matter what would happen to my business in bad times or good times, those checks **had** to be sent before paying our own mortgage. I'm not sure, but perhaps that's why I would constantly work day and night at full speed since these people became dependent on my income.

Once I started to get involved with local organizations and charities, I found myself working even harder, refusing to think

Lemon Juice

about not sending checks to those that needed it more than our own needs.

Every time that I had an excellent financial reward from an investment I had made, the first thought in my mind would be 'what organization can I find that can put this money to its best use?'

In interviews on television and in newspapers, reporters over 40 years have countless times asked me "Why do you do it?" I would tell whoever was interviewing me that I do it because I'm selfish. I think I get more enjoyment out of seeing what I'm able to do to help someone, whether it's for a day, a week or forever, than the people that I help. I wanted to continue the legacy of my parents and grandparents who constantly helped people less fortunate than themselves. This was my familial upbringing.

Around Christmas, when my children were young, I took both of them along with my wife, Marlene, to Center City Philadelphia off Race Street where homeless people had made their refuge in 4x4 cardboard boxes.

In preparation for this visit, I had purchased 75 winter oil waxed lined raincoats, along with 75 pairs of gloves and socks. Our truck was loaded with these articles of clothing to give to the homeless.

I donned my Santa Claus outfit which I had worn the previous year when we hosted a party at our home for physically and mentally disabled children.

Epilogue

The four of us stayed together as a group as we went to each of their 'homes.' Although, finding many of them with mental issues, they refused to accept any of our gifts.

This made a lifelong impression on my children as it certainly did for Marlene and myself.

I wondered just like my grandmother had said "how can we have enough to put food on our tables and pay our bills without doing everything we can to help others that don't?"

Over the many years we have constantly 'vetted' numerous nonprofit organizations seeking those which closely matched our goals and were extremely efficient with their expenses. We wanted to be assured that the greatest amount of our donations were going to help the eventual recipients. Seeking the most efficient organizations turned into a daunting task and finding many disappointments along the way.

A vendor who periodically did work for me, had learned of our giving programs. He read about our Community College scholarship program, which has provided scholarships for those with the most financial need, remarked: "You are doing God's work." I hope I am.

I just know that "Learn, Earn and Return," is a wonderful axiom to live by. It gives me goosebumps, even today.

Looking back over the decades, I smile when I think about the old days in the car business and how there is now today the

Lemon Juice

odometer law and regulations Z: "Truth in Lending" to protect consumers.

I am proud to have conceived the program: "HireJustOne" which created 100,000 jobs when our economy was in The Great Recession. Many have said that my hiring program became the turning point for our entire economy.

The legendary newscaster and journalist, Katie Couric, when interviewing me for CBS's "Person Of The Week" program was gratified to learn how many businesses started to hire additional employees due to my innovative hiring program.

Arianna Huffington, author, businesswoman, syndicated columnist and founder of The Huffington Post, was a guest speaker at an event in Florida, telling the audience at the Emerson Center that **ONE** person can make a positive change in this world. During her speech, her eyes scanned the audience, then referring to me said: "There he is. He alone made a major difference!"

Our turkey giveaway over the years provided well over 50,000 dinners for those who would not have anything to eat if not for our program.

The "Wheelz2Work" program that I created, has produced over 450 vehicles *free* for those coming out of homelessness to get to a new job after re-training or to get to school. This program has won two National Awards from the Sam Walton Foundation.

Epilogue

I conceived and implemented "Common Ground Mission" which attracted Pennsylvania Governor Ed Rendell to be our Honorary Chairman of the Board. We sent forty two Muslim, Christians and Jewish children along with religious leaders of their faith, to Israel, all expenses paid, to see for themselves how the three religions started within feet of each other and the commonality that we all have. It gained national exposure on the news and was instrumental in promoting peace and understanding between the faiths.

Thirty years ago, yet another reporter asked me what would best sum up my life. He wanted to know what I would like placed on my grave marker. I thought about it for a moment and replied: **"Tough, but caring."** I believe that succinctly sums up my personality.

Not giving up paying back, I met with people at the University of Pittsburgh Medical Center [UPMC] to find if their transplant unit had any unfulfilled needs. I was informed there was one was facet which was urgent. There were patients who received organ transplants but could not afford to pay their monthly deductibles because of financial difficulties, so due to the cost, they were skipping their anti-rejection medication. This was a major problem for them. I took care of it by giving them a $50,000 check and raised another $86,000 in their community to fund this need. One affluent recipient heard about my program and promised to fund it in perpetuity...

The irony to me is that even as a young kid I would do almost anything to help out others. But, I really wasn't able to do it

Lemon Juice

fully without the profits that I made buying and selling new and used cars.

I did plenty of things that upset me but looking back at everything and the end results, given the choice of not doing anything, I would do it all over again.

I hope you enjoyed reading some of the unique and noteworthy adventures in my life. There still may be more to come.

Stay tuned.